The Power of Institutions

*Checks & Balances — Credible Commitment by
Constraints — Stability*

vs

*Decisive Leadership — capacity to be flexible
& avoid Gridlock & fragmentation
— Woodrow Wilson on USA : late C19
— OLSON on UK Parliamentary system — 1970s*

Diagrams — pp 30-31

A volume in the series

Cornell Studies in Political Economy

EDITED BY PETER J. KATZENSTEIN

A full list of titles in the series appears at the end of the book.

The Power of Institutions

POLITICAL ARCHITECTURE AND GOVERNANCE

ANDREW MACINTYRE

CORNELL UNIVERSITY PRESS

Ithaca and London

First published 2003 by Cornell University Press
First printing, Cornell Paperbacks, 2003

Printed in the United States of America

Library of Congress Cataloging-in-Publication Data

MacIntyre, Andrew J., 1960–
    The power of institutions : political architecture and governance / Andrew MacIntyre.
        p. cm. — (Cornell studies in political economy)
    Includes bibliographical references and index.
    ISBN 0-8014-4051-3 (cloth : alk. paper)—ISBN 0-8014-8799-4 (pbk. : alk. paper)
    1. Political planning—Asia, Southeastern—Case studies. 2. Asia, Southeastern—Politics and government—1945—Case studies. I. Title. II. Series.
    JQ750.A56 P645 2003
    320'.6'0959—dc21   2002007944

Cloth printing   10 9 8 7 6 5 4 3 2 1

Paperback printing   10 9 8 7 6 5 4 3 2 1

To the memory of
Sigmond K. Schwartz
1913−1999

An American trader who thought about Asia
and cared about scholarship.
And a fine old friend who liked to lunch.

Contents

Preface

This is a book about political form. It explores the way national politics is structured and some of the implications of this for the quality of governance. It is concerned with the configuration of formal political institutions and what the implications of this are for the management of policy. The book grows in part out of my puzzlement over a little-discussed tension in the sprawling literature about the effects of political institutions. Two well-developed ideas that emerge from this literature pull in opposite directions. One points to the virtues of political frameworks that disperse the control of national decision making, whereas the other points to the virtues of political frameworks that unify national decision making. The tension between these two ideas and the respective bodies of thought that lie behind them has intrigued me for some time.

This book develops an argument that reconciles them. I argue that it is useful to think in terms of a power concentration paradox, according to which we can find characteristic and increasingly problematic governance syndromes the further we move toward the extremes—whether in the direction of concentrating or fragmenting institutional authority. In other words, national political frameworks that either severely concentrate or severely fragment decision-making power are prone to characteristic (albeit quite different) governance problems. And, interestingly, as we move toward either end of the range, it is developing-country polities that we are most likely to encounter.

ix

This is a book that grows in part out of my curiosity about contending ideas, but it also grows out of my curiosity about developing countries and, in particular, the world of Southeast Asia, which I follow with an abiding fascination. Watching the way in which the differently configured Southeast Asian states have wrestled in distinct ways with common problems has exercised my interest over the years, as have the tremendous struggles in recent times over the basic rules organizing political life. Political scientists have had much to say about the importance of institutions in advanced industrial democracies, but much less about institutions in developing countries, especially in Southeast Asia. I hope to help change this. I focus on elements of the political histories of Indonesia, Malaysia, the Philippines, and Thailand, both for their own sakes, and to make wider statements about the implications of institutional configuration for governance.

This is a book that maps the author's intellectual evolution particularly closely. My original fascination with Indonesia and then with other Southeast Asian states, my interest in detailed and applied analysis of the way these various states are put together, and the importance of this for the way they behave and interact with one another, all reflect my Australian origins and training. One of my primary professional motives in coming to the United States and the University of California, San Diego (UCSD), was to try my luck at a different scholarly table, where the game gave more emphasis to determined comparativism rather than deep case immersion. The attempt to work across four country cases and the tight focus on formal political institutions and their consequences reflect my years at UCSD. In many ways, this book comes out of the San Diego school of institutional analysis and seeks to help export this to the world of developing countries and Southeast Asia in particular. But the arrows flow in the other direction too. Rather than focus tightly on electoral systems or some other important but very specific institutional variable, I push for a macro perspective in thinking about the broader implications of the institutional configuration at the national level for the overall pattern of policy management. And I seek to step beyond what is, relatively speaking, the neat and tidy analytical world of stable and advanced industrial democracies to embrace the analytically slippery and volatile world of developing-country politics.

The evolution and development of this book have been much aided by suggestions and support from a wide network of colleagues in San Diego and further afield. I need to thank several people specifically. Martin Beversdorf, William Case, Peter Gourevitch, Stephan Haggard, Allen Hicken, Chalmers Johnson, Matthew Shugart, John Sidel, and Nancy Viviani were all good enough to wade through the initial draft of the manuscript and to offer me very thorough and helpful critiques. At different times and in different ways Emil Bolongaita, Jean Blondel, Rick Doner, Don Emmerson, Miles Kahler, Dwight King, David Lake, David McKendrick, John McMillan, Barry Naughton, Greg Noble, T. J. Pempel, Dick Robison, Phil Roeder, Peter Timmer, and Meredith Woo-Cummings helped me with key insights and encouragement. In Southeast Asia, many people helped over an extended period, but discussions with Suchit Bunbongkarn, Noel de Dios, Edward Terrence Gomez, and Andi Mallarangeng were particularly helpful.

At Cornell University Press, two reviewers and Peter Katzenstein offered unusually engaged and constructive critiques, which aided the book greatly. And the long-celebrated dynamic duo of Roger Haydon and Peter Katzenstein made the review and publication process wonderfully efficient through straight-dealing, judiciously timed bursts of encouragement, and much appreciated advice.

Martin Beversdorft, Allen Hicken, and Yuko Kasuya provided marvellous research assistance, and, on top of all her other activities, Kay-Marie Johns helped me with the rapid and cheery preparation of the manuscript. Primary funding for the research underlying the volume came from the Smith Richardson Foundation, which is warmly acknowledged, as is the oversight of the project by first Samantha Ravich and then Al Song.

To all these people—as well as others not named here—I express my appreciation and gratitude. But it is the smiles of Julia and Alex, Charlotte, and Oliver that make it all worthwhile.

Andrew MacIntyre

San Diego, California

CHAPTER 1

Power by Design

Some of the most fiercely fought political battles in developing countries today are about how national politics should be organized. Policy struggles over who gets what are the routine stuff of politics. Battles over the structure and process of politics, in a sense the when and how of politics, are more fundamental. Politicians and politically mobilized sections of society intuitively recognize that the rules of the political game can have a powerful bearing on policy outcomes. The basic organizational rules of national politics matter in all countries, but they are particularly consequential in developing countries, where social, economic, and political ferment is often greatest. From Russia to South Africa to Venezuela, we have seen efforts in the recent past to alter some or other aspect of the basic rules of political life in ways that reshape the national political architecture.

National political architecture is merely a metaphor to capture the complex totality of a country's basic political institutions—the rules, usually enshrined in a constitution and other key laws, that determine how the leadership of a state is configured and how state authority is exercised. These are foundational issues in politics. This is a book about the extent to which national political architecture concentrates or disperses governmental decision-making power. Is control over decision making to be centralized in the hands of a small number of players—perhaps even just one person—or is it to be dispersed more widely? This, of course, is a timeless theme among philosophers, stretching back at least to the ancient Greeks. My concerns are more concrete and contemporary. I am interested in exploring the way in which different institutional frameworks concentrate or disperse power and the consequences of this for a country's overall pattern of governance. This connects to some of the most basic challenges in politics, and it also connects to unresolved problems in scholarly theorizing about institutions and governance.

Institutions are constraints that shape behavior in all sorts of areas of human activity, stretching from social interaction to economic exchange to international cooperation. This study can thus be situated within a much wider body of scholarship concerned with the origins, design, and consequences of institutions, one that spans economics, sociology, philosophy, and history as much as political science. Within political science, much research has focused tightly on particular institutional features (e.g., electoral systems) and their effect on particular political phenomena (e.g., how voters behave or how politicians organize themselves for the purpose of winning office). And, overwhelmingly, research has been conducted in the context of advanced industrial democracies. This study differs in both respects. I take a wider-angle perspective, examining overall political architecture as framed by the interaction of the constitutional structure of national government and the party system, the extent to which this political architecture concentrates or disperses power, and the implications of this for the prevailing pattern of policy management. Further, I build and illustrate my central claims on the basis of four country cases from Southeast Asia—Thailand, the Philippines, Malaysia, and Indonesia—and generalize these claims to developing countries. This speaks to my two core objectives: to extend the theoretical debate about the consequences of formal political institutions and to illuminate some of the most important contemporary political issues in Southeast Asia and, indeed, in developing countries more broadly. In so doing, I also hope to help bring the study of Southeast Asian politics back into the mainstream of political science, from which it has been oddly estranged for nearly a generation.

At the most basic level, this study is motivated by a simple question: What difference, if any, does the extent of dispersal of governmental decision-making power make? The lively debate through the 1990s about the advantages and disadvantages of presidential and parliamentary forms of government captured some of this variation, but by no means all.[1] Issues such as whether the head of government is separately elected from the legislature, although prominent, are by no means the only significant points of variation among political frameworks. Indeed, it quickly becomes apparent that there are countless possible institutional configurations once we reflect on the full range of variation of factors such as electoral systems, legislative structure, and executive powers. I do not focus just on a particular segment of the wider spectrum of existing or imaginable institutional configurations. Nor, more broadly, do I limit my analysis just to the world of fully competitive democracies. Unlike so much institutionalist scholarship, I seek deliberately to include the world of semi-democracies and nondemocracies in which electoral competition is curtailed to a lesser or greater degree. In short, I am interested in the entire range of political systems, ranging from the most centralized autocracy to the most fragmented democracy. Stated simply, if we bring institutional configuration to the foreground and hold all else constant, can we say anything useful about the likely effects of the degree of concentration or dispersal of national decision-making power?

The central claim of this book is that we can indeed infer something important about the likely pattern of governance based on the gross or aggregate institutional characteristics of a country's political system. And, in so doing, we can extend the theoretical debate about the effects of institutions on governance in useful ways. In my initial efforts to interrogate the literature on institutions and governance, I was struck forcefully by a basic theoretical cleavage. On one hand, there is a well-established and influential school of thought arguing the dangers of centralized political systems. This literature stresses the importance of institutional arrangements that disperse power, thereby reducing the risk of arbitrary or capricious government action and making possible a stable policy environment in which governments can make policy commitments that are credible into the future. On the other hand, there is a vigorous, diverse set of argu-

1. For major contributions to this debate see, Linz and Valenzuela (1994), Lijphart (1992), Weaver and Rockman (1993), and Shugart and Carey (1992).

ments about the benefits of flexible decisive government and timely policy action. This second body of institutionalist literature underscores the way in which political fragmentation is the enemy of adaptable, responsive, and nimble government. The implications of these two perspectives pull in very different directions. One points to the dangers of political frameworks that concentrate power, the other to the dangers of political frameworks that fragment power. This is an intriguing conundrum that, strangely, has received little direct attention in the literature. I propose an argument about the effects of institutional extremes that helps to resolve this theoretical puzzle: the power concentration paradox. In building the argument, I forgo the fine-grained focus of much institutional analysis and opt for a higher level of aggregation than is usual—the gross characteristics of national political architecture as shaped by the interaction of the complex of rules that make up the constitutional structure and party system.

Consider a range along which all possible institutional configurations can be located, depending on the degree of dispersal of decision-making power. Figure 1.1 depicts this in simple terms, stretching at the left-hand end from frameworks in which decision-making power is not at all dispersed (in other words, is highly concentrated), through intermediate possibilities, and to the right-hand end to frameworks in which decision-making power is widely dispersed (in other words, highly fragmented). I argue that either extreme—that is, either heavily centralized or heavily fragmented frameworks—are particularly susceptible to problematic patterns of governance. Further, these problematic patterns of governance contrast starkly and are specific to one or the other institutional extreme. Countries whose national political architecture produces a highly centralized decision-making structure are susceptible to a very changeable or volatile pattern of policy management. Conversely, at the other extreme, countries whose political architecture produces a highly fragmented

Low	Medium	High
(concentrated)		(fragmented)

Figure 1.1 Dispersal of Decision-Making Power

4

decision-making structure are susceptible to an inflexible or rigid pattern of policy management.

This argument has implications for all polities, but I contend that the underlying logic is likely to have particular bite for developing countries. This may seem a surprising proposition; conventional wisdom flowing from Max Weber onward associates stable and meaningful institutions with entrenched democracy. The significance of institutions in developing countries is often discounted because the rule of law is typically weak, with some governments being in a position to bend the judiciary in any direction desired. How can rules of any sort be important if the legal system is weak and has little independence from the government? Part of the answer is that the very notion of a standardized norm about the rule of law is itself problematic. There is in fact considerable variation even among countries with established legal systems in the legal position of the state and the political authority of the judiciary.[2] But more than this, not all institutions are dependent on enforcement by an independent judiciary or third party. The elemental effects of a country's national political architecture in configuring decision-making power can be starkly apparent even in situations in which the legal system is weak and impedes complex institutions, such as a stock exchange.

The deepening and development of a country's legal system is certainly integral to the deepening and development of the wider web of institutions that we observe in advanced industrial democracies. But this by no means implies that the absence of a strong and fully independent judiciary precludes the possibility that the basic elements of constitutional structure and party system shape political life. Very few semidemocracies and nondemocracies are utterly formless or unstructured politically. Pure autocracies are very rare. In nearly all authoritarian polities there is in fact a range of formal and informal rules that political actors play by and that thus shape politics in important ways. We get powerful illustrations of this from communist systems. Work on China and the former Soviet Union by Susan Shirk and Philip Roeder, respectively, has highlighted the way in which political institutions shape outcomes in strikingly nondem-

2. Clark (1999); Jayasuriya (1999).

ocratic systems in which notions of judicial independence simply do not pertain.[3] More broadly, we can also see this point illustrated historically in the origins of political frameworks to replace absolute monarchies in Europe. The emergence of institutional frameworks that empowered parliaments rested not on independent judiciaries but on power-sharing bargains or truces forged among pivotal elements of the political elite, together with the nature of the external security environment.[4] Similarly, we know that in imperial China key elements of the power structure were highly institutionalized without the presence of an independent legal authority.[5] Strong and independent legal systems do indeed facilitate the development of complex institutional arrangements, but weak legal systems do not negate the possibility of consequential national political architecture.

In studies of politics in advanced industrial democracies, institutional explanations are widespread; it is taken for granted that "institutions matter" in myriad ways. But in studies of the developing world, the position of formal political institutions as a standard explanatory variable is much more tenuous. This is a mistake. There are a number of reasons for suspecting that national political architecture is in fact particularly consequential for developing countries. The political frameworks of developing countries are more likely to be located toward the extremes of our range of institutional configurations. Typically, advanced industrial democracies are located toward the center of this range and are thus less susceptible to stark differentiation on the basis of the extent of centralization alone. But consider for a moment the much more diverse world of developing-country polities. Developing countries are much more likely to be located toward the extremes of the range, either because democracy is weak or nonexistent and power is therefore heavily centralized in the executive or, conversely, in those that are democratic, because party systems are more likely to be fluid and fragmented, thereby increasing wide dispersal of decision-making power across fractionated legislative coalitions.[6]

3. Shirk (1992); Roeder (1993).
4. North and Weingast (1989); Root (1994); Ertman (1997).
5. Miller (2000); Bartlett (1991); Schram (1987).
6. Scott Mainwaring (1999) has done much to open up the study of the dynam-

6

Not only are developing-country polities more likely to be located away from the center and toward the extremes, but the character of the wider political environment accentuates the matter. The overall formal institutional landscape in developing countries is typically much sparser, and this makes the configuration of government especially consequential. In advanced industrial democracies we see a thick web of social and economic regulatory institutions, such as an independent judiciary, a free press, and independent regulatory agencies (central banks, antimonopoly commissions, telecommunication commissions, electoral commissions, stock markets, aviation authorities, patent authorities, ombudsmen, and so on). Together, institutions such as these serve as countervailing forces to government, delimiting the areas in which it has effective discretion and in varying degrees helping society monitor and constrain government. Unlike their developing-country counterparts, governments in those few OECD (Organization for Economic Cooperation and Development) countries that do feature very centralized political frameworks are constrained by a thick web of other institutions that reduces the scope for arbitrary or capricious behavior. Britain and (until the 1990s) New Zealand are the prime examples of this, with highly centralized political frameworks permitting very flexible and decisive policy action, but with governments also constrained by a surrounding web of social and economic institutions minimizing the scope for the sort of arbitrary action that similarly highly centralized governments in developing countries can display. We can extend this argument beyond economic and social institutional constraints to constraints emanating from civil society itself. The range and strength of associational life is typically less extensive in the developing world than the OECD world, where myriad nonstate actors are actively involved in monitoring and contesting policy. Although an emerging force in many developing countries, associations and other nonstate actors are or have been dependent in some measure on the state.

---

ics of party systems in developing, as distinct from advanced industrial, democracies through his work on Brazil. Allen Hicken (1999, 2002) extends this line of inquiry in new directions, focusing on the connection between party systems and policy outcomes and using southeast Asian cases. More generally, see Haggard and Kaufman (1995).

In short, both because their national political architecture is more likely to be located toward the extremes and because this architecture is less likely to be enmeshed in a thick web of other social and economic institutions, developing countries are more likely to be susceptible to either of the problematic patterns of governance—policy volatility and policy rigidity—that severely centralized and severely fragmented political frameworks generate. And further still, these distinctive policy syndromes are likely to be particularly costly in developing countries. Ultimately, this is because the role played by government is, on average, so much more consequential in developing countries. We can illustrate this from various angles. In economic terms, because capital markets and the private sector more generally are much less developed, the state plays a much more pivotal role in mobilizing and directing resources. This is not simply a matter of the size of government spending or state enterprises—there is in fact considerable variation along this dimension among both developed and developing countries—but, more subtly, the extent to which policy affects economic outcomes. Quite apart from normative debates about the appropriate policy posture for developing countries, in part because government looms so large, it has great potential for economic good and for economic harm.[7] Another way of viewing this is to recognize that the policy burden on developing-country governments is typically much higher than on advanced industrial democracies. Because the range and scale of problems confronting developing countries are so great—running from widespread poverty and basic problems of public health and education to the maintenance of rudimentary law, order, and national security—even more turns on the ability of the government to address them than is typically the case in OECD countries. Government is, of course, important everywhere, but in developing countries its actions have greater potential to both help and harm.

Let us turn now from these broad considerations about the salience of national political architecture back to the central thesis

7. Work by Jeffrey Sachs and Andrew Warner (1995) highlighting the much greater variance of economic growth rates among developing countries and likely connections with national policy environments offers a partial window onto this elusive reality.

of this study and consider the research design on which it rests. To reiterate, the primary argument of this book is that the configuration of a country's basic political institutions (growing largely out of its constitutional structure and party system) has important implications for its basic pattern of governance. This is not an argument about how institutions affect the substance or content of policy but rather how they affect the form of policy or, more broadly, the pattern of policy management. Political frameworks that either severely concentrate or severely fragment decision-making power are susceptible to serious—albeit starkly contrasting—problems. The former are prone to policy volatility and the latter to policy rigidity. Either of these syndromes is likely to engender serious problems over time. To illustrate and support these deductive inferences, I offer detailed analytical narratives from four Southeast Asian case studies. I trace the way in which governments in Thailand, the Philippines, Malaysia, and Indonesia responded to a common policy challenge—containing the economic crisis of 1997–98—and link the overall pattern of policy management exhibited by each back to that country's institutional framework.

The results are striking. The four cases are strongly differentiated along the independent or explanatory variable. Thailand's national political architecture produced a severely fragmented political configuration; Malaysia's and, even more so, Indonesia's produced heavily centralized configurations; and the Philippines's produced a more intermediate configuration. Figure 1.2 describes this graphically by locating each of the cases on our one-dimensional range of the degree of dispersal of decision-making power in political frameworks. (For now, suspend questions about measurement; we will come to this in chap. 2.)

The spread is no less interesting on the outcome side. During the economic crisis of 1997–98, Thailand was gripped by debilitating

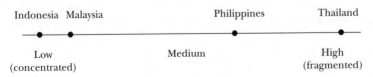

Figure 1.2 Dispersal of Decision-Making Power circa 1997

policy rigidity and proved unable to respond in anything like a timely matter. In stark contrast, Malaysia and, even more so, Indonesia exhibited the opposite syndrome—a policy environment that was highly changeable and unpredictable. Both extremes were severely problematic. Although the Philippines certainly struggled in crafting a response to the crisis, it was able to present a steady position, adjusting when necessary in a tolerably timely fashion. I argue that it is no coincidence that the broad pattern of policy behavior we see exhibited in each case corresponds strongly with the predictions of my institutional model.

These four case studies are offered as primary evidence illustrating my thesis about the implications of extreme configurations in national political architecture. I also present evidence of another sort by examining the overall pattern and direction of institutional change in these countries. Again, the history of these four Southeast Asian cases has much to tell us. In Southeast Asia—as in many parts of the developing world—politics has been changing shape in recent times. This is not just a story of democratization—although that is often part of it. More subtly and elusively, it is a question of institutional design and the implications of institutions for governance. By the close of the twentieth century, political reform had become a hot issue across these Southeast Asian countries—albeit with quite different effects. In a second set of case studies, I trace the diverse struggles over the possibility of reforming the national political architectures of Thailand, the Philippines, Malaysia, and Indonesia. This second set of case studies flows conveniently from the first because the economic trauma of the 1997–98 financial crisis played powerfully into debates over political reform.

The findings from this second set of comparative case studies are no less striking. To foreshadow some of the results, we see the outlier cases moving in from the institutional extremes. Thailand and Indonesia, our two cases with the most severely fragmented and centralized institutional configurations, respectively, underwent a process of institutional reconfiguration that had the effect of pulling them in from the extremes on our continuum of institutional forms. Further, although the public debates surrounding reform were multidimensional, there was a clear recognition of the governance problems associated with the existing political architecture. No less revealing are the stories of the defeat of the campaign for political change in Malaysia and the Philippines. I certainly do not suggest that there is any neat and tidy teleological pattern of convergence here—the cases highlight far too many contingencies to entertain such notions. What this second set of cases does show us is the extent to which extreme political configurations were seen to have failed and that amid all the other objectives that were swept up at a moment of possible political change there was a strong determination to redesign the national political architecture in such a way that it moved in from the extremes of either severe concentration or severe fragmentation.

I do not claim to have selected these cases purely on the basis of methodological considerations. To say openly, with Robert Bates and colleagues, that the cases in effect selected me rather than the other way around probably is closer to the truth.[8] In varying degrees, these four countries have been a source of enduring and compelling fascination for me. I work with them here not because I chose them dispassionately but because I know something about them. Having said this, it is also happily the case that these four cases lend themselves very handily to my analytic purposes in seeking to highlight the effects of institutions on governance.

The danger of focusing the spotlight on institutions is, of course, that in so doing we might obscure the impact of other variables, thereby exaggerating the causal significance of institutions. It is therefore important to consider the other likely suspects. Reduced to their essence, the other primary causal drivers that political scientists routinely consider are interests, ideas, and international systemic forces.

Methodologically, the appeal of these four Southeast Asian cases is that they allow us in large measure to control for the possible independent effects of these other factors during the period under consideration. They allow me to approximate a controlled comparison using most similar cases. All four countries have historically had primarily commodity-based economies, moving forward in the latter part of the twentieth century with the development of sizable manu-

8. Bates et al. (1998, 13).

facturing sectors, including industries that can compete in world markets. To be sure, there are some differences in the details of the timing and pace of their developmental spurts as well as their particular sectoral endowments, but by the mid-1990s we can see them all having broadly comparable coalitions of economic interests underlying government. Similarly, in terms of basic ideas, through the 1990s we can see them all pursuing broadly comparable economic policy orientations. All sought to foster rapid economic growth based on generally orthodox macroeconomic policy and trade and investment policies that were largely liberal in nature—although certainly leavened with selective assistance for certain firms and industries. And in terms of international systemic considerations, not only does their close geographic proximity mean that they all shared the same neighborhood or subregional environment, but, further, their fundamental economic and security dispositions toward the major powers (the United States, Japan, China, and Europe) were essentially comparable. In short, it is not obviously the case that there are fundamental differences among the cases in terms of their underlying structure of economic interests, the prevailing climate of ideas about national policy, or their location within the wider international economic and security systems. These basic commonalities all facilitate my study. They make it reasonable for me to proceed as if other things could be held constant and to bring political institutions to the foreground in explaining broad patterns of governance.

Ultimately this book is built around a deductive argument supported by two sets of comparative cases. There is, of course, a variety of other ways that the task of assembling empirical evidence might have been approached, ranging from a fine-grain detailed approach of the single-country case study to a large-n statistical analysis detached from any particular country or region. My approach of working in two cuts with four detailed cases represents something of an intermediate strategy, although clearly one that leans in a qualitative direction. Attempting to undertake serious qualitative research across these four country case studies is extremely costly. It is no accident that monographic research on Southeast Asian politics has overwhelmingly taken the form of single-country studies. This reflects both the distinct traditions of scholarship on the various countries and the linguistic diversity among them. But beyond the specifics of Southeast Asia–related scholarship, there are inherent methodological trade-offs here. As a matter of principle, the single-country specialist is reluctant to forgo empirical detail and completeness and, conversely, the general comparativist is reluctant to pass up the external validation of theoretical claims by robust statistical analysis of a much larger set of polities. Methodological strategy is almost always substantially path-dependent; we are seldom free to adopt a strategy that departs radically from earlier choices or investments we have made in particular analytical technologies or, more broadly, approaches to scholarship. We can make some adjustment, but rarely radical adjustment. The approach I take here seeks to balance the ability to convincingly trace causality on the basis of detailed casework with the analytic leverage afforded by contrasting cases that vary along the dimensions of theoretical interest, but that are otherwise reasonably comparable. Working with only a small handful of cases, this is inevitably much more an exercise in theory building than theory testing. My goal is to combine deductive inference and solid empirical illustration to throw light on a largely unexplored set of questions about institutions and governance.

This book is intended for two audiences: one with general theoretical interests in institutions and governance, particularly in the developing world, and one interested in Southeast Asia for its own sake. Finding a balance that enables me to serve both audiences has been perhaps the single greatest challenge in writing this book. Over and over again I have come up against difficult decisions on the appropriate level of elaboration. What one constituency may find unremarkable the other may find controversial or intriguing, and vice versa. At root, this is because the leading specialist literature on Southeast Asian politics has been remarkably uninterested in institutional issues. Instead, the causal factors that have captured the imaginations of most scholarly observers of politics in Southeast Asia have had much more to do with either interests or ideas than with institutions. Although a simplification of a rich and diverse literature, it is striking how much of the leading literature on Southeast Asia is concerned with either the consequences of interests (e.g., class interests, industry-specific interests, ethnic interests, regional interests, or just factional interests) or ideational issues (e.g., identity, conceptions of nation, or conceptions of freedom and responsibility).[9] And such attention as has been given to political institutions has typically been cast at a very macrolevel, with notions of state capacity and relative state autonomy or broad forms of interest representation such as clientelism and corporatism.[10] There has been very little attention given to the formal institutional variables that I term national political architecture. Beyond very broad-gauge contrasts between democratic and nondemocratic regimes, there has been little attention paid to the great differences in the way in which national politics is organized among these countries. The interesting partial exception to this is the small but growing body of public intellectual discourse by Southeast Asian political observers, who are often less concerned with grand scholarly discourse and more interested in trying to shape political debates in their own countries.

In the mid-1980s, there was little sustained research on formal political institutions in Latin America. Indeed, those who pioneered this research in Latin America had to endure the disdain of a scholarly mainstream that was accustomed to focusing on other explanatory variables. Today, not only is the analysis of formal political institutions very much a mainstream preoccupation, important institutionalist theorizing of much wider application comes from the study of Latin American cases. More recently, a similar pattern can be seen in scholarship on Eastern Europe. In part, this trend no doubt reflects greater democratization. The importance of political institutions becomes more apparent and more extensive with de-

9. Some of the most interesting exemplars include Robison (1987), Suehiro (1989), Jesudason (1989), Rivera (1994), Gomez and Jomo (1997), Pasuk and Baker (1998), and Sidel (1999b) for interest-centered accounts and Acharya (2001), Anderson (1990), Tongchai (1994), Khoo (1995), Emmerson (1995), Kahn (1998), and Kelly and Reid (1998) for ideas-centered accounts. Approaches of this sort have crowded out institutional perspectives, but even more starkly neglected are what might be termed international systemic approaches, which emphasize the causal significance of the global security structure for policy. One of the few good exemplars of this for Southeast Asia is Stubbs (1999).

10. See for example, Doner (1991, 1992), Bowie (1991), Anek (1992), Yoshihara (1988), Hutchcroft (1998), Hadiz (1999), and MacIntyre (1991, 1994).

mocratization; indeed, some of the variables of greatest interest to institutionalist theorists—for instance, electoral rules—may have little relevance in nondemocratic settings. But it is a mistake to believe that this is true of all institutional variables. As I have already argued, even in weakly democratic and nondemocratic regimes there are usually well-understood rules about which actors have decision-making authority.

I hope to call the attention of the Southeast Asia research community to the exciting and important work of the comparative institutionalist research community. And in so doing, I also aim to help open up an institutionalist research frontier centered on Southeast Asia. I seek to highlight the remarkable variation in the organization of national politics in the region—variation that goes far beyond the simple distinction between democratic and nondemocratic regimes —and to highlight some of the consequences of this variation. There is an extraordinarily rich research agenda waiting here, the surface of which has only been lightly scratched.

Finally, let me quickly outline the structure of the rest of the book. The overall layout is straightforward. In chapter 2, I explore the theoretical literature on the effects of institutions on governance, seeking to convey some sense of its breadth and, more important, to highlight the basic tension between what we might term the credible commitments literature and the decisiveness literature. Having established the theoretical puzzle that lies at the core of this book, I outline my ideas for resolving it. In chapter 3, I outline the analytical device—a veto player model—I employ to compare and calibrate the diverse political frameworks that we encounter in the case studies. I then use it to specify the national political architectures of Thailand, the Philippines, Malaysia, and Indonesia—as they appeared in the mid-1990s. Chapter 4 is the first of two fully empirical chapters. It takes readers through a detailed account of the overall pattern of policy behavior in each country as the respective governments sought to battle collapsing investor confidence during the regional economic crisis of 1997–98. In each case, I link the pattern of policy management to the institutional framework and thus back to the theoretical claims in chapter 2, arguing that the various patterns of behavior displayed were very much in keeping with the predictions of my model. Chapter 5 takes readers a step further, exploring the substance and direction of ensuing episodes of successful and aborted institutional change across our four Southeast Asian case studies. These narratives point to a broad pattern of institutional reform that ties back strongly to my central argument about the effects of the heavy concentration or fragmentation of decision-making authority. The concluding chapter reflects on what has been gained in terms of ideas about institutions and governance, as well as in terms of applications to politics in Southeast Asia. More broadly, it also reflects on the strengths and limitations of institutional perspectives on politics.

CHAPTER 2

The Power Concentration Paradox

In this chapter, I briefly explore the relevant literature to draw out what we already know about the effects of institutions on governance and to highlight the underlying opposition that divides much of the existing theorizing on the subject. I then establish this theoretical conundrum as the central puzzle of the rest of the book and outline my argument for resolving it: the power concentration paradox.

CURRENT THEORIES ABOUT POLITICAL INSTITUTIONS AND GOVERNANCE

The study of institutions is not new; there have been several earlier waves of interest in the subject. In the early 1980s, for instance, an important body of work argued for the primacy of institutional form over the nature or substance of particular policy problems or sectors. At that time, the battle advanced the idea that the politics of a particular problem—say, health care—was not the same the world over (or, at least, was not the same the industrial world over) but was powerfully conditioned by the particular form of a country's political institutions.[1] The focus of later debate has shifted. The emphasis was

1. The benchmark work was the series Comparative Policy and Politics in Industrial States stewarded by Douglas Ashford, Peter Katzenstein, and T. J. Pempel. See, inter alia, Ashford (1981), Pempel (1982), and Katzenstein (1988).

more on advancing the independent effects of institutions as opposed to other causal factors (such as interests) and, more important, on attempts to theorize the effects of particular institutional features in generalizable ways. There is now a sizable literature in this direction, growing out of both economics and political science; within political science it crosses several fields: American politics, comparative politics, and international relations. Connecting much of it, however, is an analytical focus on the way in which institutions affect outcomes by shaping the incentives and capabilities of political and economic actors. Much of this literature is from the 1990s. It operates on both the supply side of politics, for instance, the implications of institutions for the behavior of voters in producing governments and the behavior of politicians and bureaucrats in producing policies ranging from public spending to waging war, and on the demand side, for instance, the consequences of various sorts of consumers of government policy—citizens in general, investors, international organizations, or foreign governments. Inevitably in such a sprawling and compartmentalized literature, there are many debates and subdebates. And yet, the more I read and came to appreciate the shape of the overall literary forest as distinct from its individual trees, the more I was struck by a basic divide between two currents of theorizing. One is essentially concerned with credible commitment questions and the other with what might be labeled decisiveness questions. The first focuses on the importance of a stable and dependable policy environment and the extent to which different political frameworks permit leaders to make binding policy promises that others—ordinary citizens, investors and lenders, and even potential military allies and enemies—will be able to trust. The second, by contrast, focuses on the importance of efficiency and adaptability in policy management and the extent to which different political frameworks permit leaders to respond in a timely fashion to changing local and international circumstances and needs.

This is an unusual way to categorize or dissect the literature, yet doing so yields important insights. Before we come to this, however, the more immediate task is to explain this theoretical dichotomy more fully.

INSTITUTIONS AND CREDIBLE COMMITMENT

The idea that institutional constraints on executive government are central to effective or good governance is a powerful one. Barry Weingast casts it as the "fundamental political dilemma," emphasizing that "a government strong enough to protect property rights is also strong enough to confiscate the wealth of its citizens."[2] This is not an argument for a minimalist government (indeed, it is predicated on the notion that government has crucial tasks to perform); it is an argument for a government that is institutionally limited so that it can perform necessary tasks effectively. Although much of the theoretical debate here is very modern, it has an impressive lineage and we can readily identify much earlier encounters with elemental aspects of the issue. In different forms, this was a key concern for Hobbes, Locke, Montesquieu, Smith, Madison, and Tocqueville.[3]

Modern scholarship in this area initially sprang from the work of economists. A key element here was theoretical work on the problem of making a credible promise at one time, given the inherent risk that it may no longer be attractive to fulfill the promise at a later time. How can policy commitments made today be believable or credible tomorrow if there is nothing preventing decision makers from changing their minds? The pioneering work was Thomas Schelling's efforts in the 1960s to model strategic interaction in the context of nuclear deterrence.[4] This fed into subsequent theoretical research on bargaining, contracting, organizations, and constitutional political economy.[5] Before long, this deductive line of inquiry joined with an initially separate body of more empirical work. The path-breaking research here was that of the economic historian, Douglass North, on the importance of the emergence of stable and secure property rights regimes for the economic development of Europe in the Middle Ages.[6] Subsequent work focused more closely on the way in which

2. Weingast (1993, 287).
3. Bernholz (1993, 312–14).
4. Schelling (1960).
5. Prominent examples include Kydland and Prescott (1977), Elster (1979), Brennan and Buchanan (1985), and Williamson (1985).
6. North and Thomas (1973).

the political framework underpinned a sovereign's ability to make promises or policy commitments that were believable.[7] As North and Weingast put it:

> A ruler can establish such commitment in two ways. One is by setting a precedent of "responsible behavior," appearing to be committed to a set of rules that he or she will consistently enforce. The second is by being constrained to obey a set of rules that do not permit leeway for violating commitments. We have very seldom observed the former, in good part because the pressures and continual strain of fiscal necessity eventually led rulers to "irresponsible behavior" and the violation of agreements.[8]

Where the king's hands came to be tied by parliament, that is, where the king was forced to obtain the agreement of parliament on spending, the likelihood of arbitrary executive action was reduced in the eyes of investors. This meant that the likelihood of sovereign debt being repaid rose and thus that credit for waging war and other purposes of state became less expensive than in other polities. The introduction of new political institutions was critical to constraining the power of the political executive, which in turn provided a more stable and secure environment in which investors were less discouraged by the risk of capricious policy action. Investors could have greater confidence that sovereigns or political executives would adhere to their proclaimed policies because there were other political institutions that checked their ability to alter course. As Kenneth Shepsle pithily summarizes the general problem, "Discretion is the enemy of optimality, commitment its ally."[9]

It is not entirely coincidental that much of the work in this theoretical tradition has been undertaken by Americans; the belief in the desirability of more rather than fewer institutional constraints on executive action—checks and balances—is deeply embedded in U.S. political thought and institutions, reflecting the received wisdom of the country's colonial history and the perils of a capricious monar-

7. North and Weingast (1989); Weingast (1993); Root (1989).
8. North and Weingast (1989, 804).
9. Shepsle (1991, 246).

chy.[10] The underlying question is, however, universal: How can policy promises issued today be made credible for tomorrow?

The core idea here is simple and powerful. When political leaders enjoy wide discretion, no matter what they may promise about future policy action—achieving low inflation, meeting military alliance obligations, or adhering to International Monetary Fund (IMF) conditions for financial assistance—if their interests later require them to renege on their commitments, they will not hesitate do so. Even if a government is strongly committed to a policy to begin with, if the same policy later ceases to suit, the government will overturn it if it has the discretion to do so. Accordingly, there is no solid basis for trusting statements about the future policy environment made by governments in which decision-making power is heavily centralized. This is a serious problem because the credibility of government commitments has powerful implications for the effectiveness of policy; similar policies produce different outcomes depending on the extent to which they are believed by the relevant constituencies. There are many potential advantages to a reasonably stable and predictable policy environment. Institutions can help overcome the problem of generating credible policy commitments. If leaders are institutionally bound by the need to obtain the consent of other political actors (for instance, a parliament) in order to alter policy or if they actually deny themselves control of the issue by delegating it to a third party (for instance, an independent judiciary or an independent central bank), then it becomes more difficult for them to renege on their promises. An institutionalized division of decision-making power helps to reduce the risk of arbitrary policy action, thereby increasing the scope for credible policy promises.

The importance of institutional constraints on executive authority for enhanced credibility has been explored across many policy frontiers, from political economy to international strategy. One cluster of research examines the causal connections flowing from political institutions to policy credibility to patterns of investment and economic growth. Studies working with statistical analysis using large samples and more contextualized qualitative analyses of particular

10. For Americans, the classic repository of this thinking is the *Federalist Papers,* especially Madison's Federalist Paper no. 51.

cases have found that political frameworks that contain the risks of arbitrary governmental action are causally connected to higher rates of investment and economic growth.[11] A second broad cluster of research emphasizes the importance of credible commitments for wider macroeconomic policy considerations.[12] Yet another cluster explores the way in which national political frameworks that constrain arbitrary governmental action have powerful beneficial consequences for a state's ability to interact effectively on the international stage. Focusing on international cooperation among states, a number of authors have found that although legislative checks on the executive complicate and slow the process of negotiation, they increase the credibility of the ensuing international agreement by making its reversal less likely.[13] The World Bank has reached comparable conclusions regarding the preconditions for successful international aid programs linking multilateral lenders and national governments.[14] And still others have identified similar logics influencing the effective management of international crises and the projection of mili-

11. Henisz (2000a, 2000b) does this for investment and growth outcomes across developing and developed economies worldwide. Levy and Spiller (1996) and Bergara, Henisz, and Spiller (1998) focus on the telecommunications sector and the electricity sector worldwide, respectively, and show how political frameworks mitigating commitments problems are causally connected with higher investment rates. Borner, Brunetti, and Weder (1995) and Clague (1997) do this for economic growth rates across developing countries. Root (1996) has comparable arguments to explain the Asian economic boom. Montinola, Qian, and Weingast (1995) connect federal-like institutions with strong economic growth in China, whereas studies in Campos (2001) focus on corruption and property rights in various parts of Asia and trace causal connections between institutions enhancing policy credibility and private investment.

12. Kydland and Prescott (1977) and Calvo (1978) did early work theorizing the connection between political credibility and macroeconomic policy in general terms. Persson and Tabellini (1990, 1994) pushed these ideas further, focusing concretely on monetary and fiscal policy. And the World Bank (1997; Burki and Perry 1998) has emphasized the importance of political institutions that constrain arbitrary executive power for both policy credibility and macroeconomic reform.

13. See, for example, Cowhey (1993) on U.S.-Japanese telecom agreements, Raustiala (1997) on the international Convention on Biological Diversity, and Martin (1995, 2000) on the ratification of the European Union.

14. World Bank (1998a).

The Power Concentration Paradox

tary power, as well as the conduct of aspects of foreign policy more broadly.[15]

These sprawling clusters and subclusters of literature are quite diverse in their focus, evidence, methods, and normative preoccupations. Connecting them are the propositions that when political leaders enjoy wide discretion policy commitments are of doubtful credibility, that credibility problems are highly consequential in many spheres, and that institutional constraints on executive action can play an important role in mitigating this effect. Even though some elements remain shaky and conjectural, by the standards of social science this is a formidable body of thought and evidence.

INSTITUTIONS AND DECISIVENESS

In stark contrast to this body of literature dealing with the importance of credible commitments and the institutional underpinnings of policy stability stands a second body of inquiry concerned with adaptable government and flexibility in policy management. Policy decisiveness—the ability to tackle problems as they arise—is an important dimension of governance.[16] A broad collection of writers has focused on various institutional aspects of the differing capacities of governments to act in an adaptable or nimble way—to respond to changing circumstances in a timely fashion. Whereas some political frameworks seem to produce chronic delay and policy immobilism, others seem able to respond much more effectively and swiftly to pressing policy needs, such as undertaking major economic reform

15. On crisis management and use of force, see Fearon (1994) and Mansfield and Snyder (1995). See also Weingast (1998) on civil war. On foreign policy more broadly, see Putnam (1988) and Rogowski (1999).

16. In using the term "policy decisiveness" I am not simply referring to the single act of making a decision, but also to the much wider political process of recognizing a problem and formulating and enacting plans to deal with it. And, critically, I am focusing on the timeliness with which this takes place. For prominent examples of others using the term in this way, see Tsebelis (1995) and Cox and McCubbins (2001).

or negotiating and ratifying an international agreement. This literature is not as theoretically cohesive or as normatively focused as that dealing with credibility and policy stability. In many ways it is a more applied literature, concerned with the output of government and the practical problems of governance. It is not built around a single unifying concept, such as commitment, and there is no common vocabulary. In spite of this, it is a formidable body of scholarship and it too taps into a proud lineage of thought. It harks back to long-standing philosophical ideas and practical concerns about the character of government and effective policy leadership that can be traced back to Plato and Aristotle and to twentieth-century scholarship on the problems of governability facing both developing countries and established industrial democracies.[17] Interestingly, notwithstanding the particular attachment to an institutional separation of governmental powers in U.S. political thought, there also exists an important current of analytical and normative concern about fragmentation and gridlock that periodically comes to the fore. The classic exemplar of this is Woodrow Wilson's despairing late-nineteenth-century account of U.S. government (written when he was still a mere political scientist).[18] This has been a persistent concern, finding subsequent embodiment in the push for constitutional reform in the second half of the twentieth century amid chronic problems of divided government.[19]

The contemporary literature concerned explicitly or implicitly with decisiveness and policy flexibility and its institutional foundations is quite diverse. One cluster deals with questions of state autonomy and state strength. Some of the leading work in this vein was an intellectual reaction against the interests-based theories of pluralists and Marxists alike, as well as against the modest developmental role prescribed for the state by liberal economists. For Theda Skocpol and others, the push for a more state-centered perspective is, in part, an effort to demonstrate the state's potential as an agent

17. See, for instance, the widely read work of the 1960s and 1970s by Huntington and others (Huntington 1968; Crozier, Huntington, and Watanuki 1975).

18. Wilson (1885).

19. For an overview of the history and debates about constitutional reform in the United States, see Sundquist (1992).

for major economic and political change.[20] Others, such as Peter Katzenstein and Stephen Krasner, have been struck by the apparent ability of industrial democracies that featured a concentration of power in the executive branch of government to respond much more rapidly and effectively to common policy problems, such as the oil crisis of the 1970s.[21] Still others have focused on the political economy of development and on the way some strong states (with more or less authoritarian political frameworks) seemed to insulate key policy agencies, enabling them to withstand diversionary pressures from other political and economic actors that would normally block major policy reform.[22] Much of this work focused on East and then Southeast Asia. Running through much of this literature is a focus on institutional capabilities and the way in which states of the high-growth Asian economies seem much more able to mobilize resources, make difficult decisions in response to changing circumstances, and carry out far-reaching economic reform to foster investment and facilitate export-oriented industrialization.

Whereas this first cluster of research focuses on institutional characteristics of decisiveness at a quite macrolevel (the nature of the state as a whole), a separate but logically parallel research effort focuses at a more microlevel, dissecting the formal institutional foundations of various political frameworks. Key variables here have been electoral systems, the institutional division of governmental powers, the nature of the party system, and the nature of bureaucratic delegation. One of the important themes in this literature is the way in which fragmentation and dispersal of power stemming from the interplay of constitutional structure and the character of the party system leads to policy delay, gridlock, and immobilism. The more widely the control of policy is dispersed—between executive and legislative branches, among political parties, between houses of the legislature, between

20. Evans, Rueschemeyer, and Skocpol (1985).

21. Katzenstein (1976, 1978); Krasner (1978). See also Zysman (1983).

22. There is a very large literature in this vein. See, for instance, Johnson (1982), Deyo (1987), Haggard (1990), Wade (1990), Amsden (1990) Woo (1991), Doner (1992), MacIntyre and Jayasuriya (1992), MacIntyre (1994), Hutchcroft (1998), and Woo-Cummings (1999).

national and subnational levels of government, between judicial and political branches, and so on—the greater the propensity to delay or avoid policy action involving sacrifice and high political costs.[23]

Much research has explored the way in which particular institutional features serve to unify or divide political actors and decision-making authority.[24] In addition to this more general research, there has also been extensive exploration of the way in which institutional frameworks that fragment decision-making authority create problems for timely and coherent policy management in specific issue areas. This embraces both theoretically oriented work by economists and political scientists and more applied work by substantive policy specialists. Important exemplars come from work on fiscal policy and the management of budgetary processes, social welfare spending, health-care reform, and foreign policy.[25] On a broader scale and

23. Key synoptic studies here are Weaver and Rockman (1993), Tsebelis (1995), and Cox and McCubbins (2001). Mayhew (1991) offers a dissenting opinion, arguing that divided partisan control of government in the United States has had no significant effect on legislative productivity. Others counter that such a claim rests on a very particular approach to the metrics of legislative output. Also noteworthy here as a divergent, if not dissenting, view is Lijphart's (1984, 1999) thesis on the virtues of consensual government, in which power is spread broadly among political, economic, and social actors. But this is much wider ranging and does not contradict the core notion that greater dispersal of formal decision-making authority makes policy change slower and more difficult.

24. On the impact of different electoral systems on the number of political parties and their cohesiveness, see, for instance, Duverger (1954), Rae (1971), Cain, Ferejohn, and Fiorina (1987), Carey and Shugart (1995), and Cox (1997). On the effect of presidential as opposed to parliamentary forms of government, see Linz and Valenzuela (1994), Lijphart (1992), and Shugart and Mainwaring (1997). On variation among presidential systems and its effects, see Shugart and Carey (1992), Carey and Shugart (1998), and Haggard and McCubbins (2001). On the effect of unicameral, as opposed to bicameral, legislatures, see Riker (1992) and Tsebelis and Money (1997). And on variation among party systems, see Sartori (1976), Laver and Schofield (1991), and Mainwaring and Scully (1995).

25. On budgets and fiscal policy, see Roubini and Sachs (1989), Grilli, Masciandaro, and Tabellini (1991), McCubbins (1991), Alt and Lowry (1994), and Poterba (1994). On welfare spending, see Huber, Ragin, and Stephens (1993); and on health care see Immergut (1992), Maioni (1998), and Marmor (1994). In the realm of foreign policy, see Milner (1997) on negotiating and ratifying agreements for international cooperation, as well as Avant (1994), Auerswald (1999), and Brooks (1999) on the development of military doctrine and the conduct of war.

picking upon the experiences of developing countries, comparable conclusions have been reached in studies on economic reform and crisis management.[26]

Running through much of this literature is attention to the way that certain institutional features promote or hinder flexible policy action by governments. Countries in which, for instance, the electoral system produces weak or incoherent parties and multiparty coalitions or in which the structure of government produces fragmented authority among multiple decision-making bodies are likely to be slow to reform and have difficulty responding to policy challenges that demand prompt focused action. Whether reforming policy to create an attractive environment for investors, responding to some pressing local welfare need, or negotiating and implementing an international agreement with the IMF or foreign governments, the extent to which a country's political framework permits policy flexibility can have major consequences.

THE PROBLEM

I have characterized the institutionalist scholarship in terms of two contrasting currents of theorizing that I have assembled under the labels of credible commitments and decisiveness. There is a powerful tension here—commitments-type arguments pull in the opposite direction from decisiveness-type arguments. Not only do the governance qualities that they each prize—policy stability and policy flexibility, respectively—sharply contrast, so too do the institutional foundations that give rise to them. Other things being equal, policy stability is maximized by an institutional framework in which control over policy is dispersed so that the likelihood of arbitrary policy action is reduced. Policy flexibility is maximized by an institutional framework in which control over policy is concentrated so that the likelihood of delay and gridlock are reduced.

Organizing the literature in this way and highlighting the underlying cleavage between commitments-type arguments and decisive-

26. Haggard and Kaufman (1992); Haggard and Webb (1994).

ness-type arguments allows us to get at basic questions about political institutions and governance in new and interesting ways. These two currents of theorizing do not stand self-consciously or conspicuously in opposition to one another. Both look at the consequences of institutions for policy and governance. Further, most—although certainly not all—scholars on both sides of the divide work within more or less rationalist approaches. Yet, curiously, the contrast between the underlying logics is seldom brought clearly into focus. Much has been missed as a result of these two bodies of literature not being joined together more often and their conflicting implications brought into prominence.

Certainly there has been some synthetic comparative analysis, but this has typically been cast in the terms of the more limited debates about the costs and benefits of Westminster-style parliamentarism versus U.S.-style presidentialism or majoritarianism versus consensus forms of government rather than in the more macro terms proposed here.[27] A few studies have explicitly recognized the underlying institutional trade-off between decisiveness and commitment. Stephan Haggard and Robert Kaufman contrast the "politics of initiation" and the "politics of consolidation," noting the different institutional requirements for major policy reform as distinct from democratic consolidation in developing countries.[28] George Tsebelis briefly discusses the precise trade-off, but remains agnostic, observing simply that whether we favor decisiveness over commitment depends on whether we prefer stability to change.[29] Gary Cox and Matthew McCubbins cast the issue in different terms, as a trade-off between state decisiveness and state resoluteness.[30] But even these few studies simply note the underlying tension rather than attempt to find a way of cutting through it.

The first objective of this book is to bring this tension squarely into focus and to call the attention of these two theoretical research communities much more fully to one another's work. For theorists, there is a conceptual puzzle here that cries out for resolution. And for the practically minded, there is a pressing real-world problem bearing di-

27. Lijphart (1992, 1999); Weaver and Rockman (1993).
28. Haggard and Kaufman (1995, 335).
29. Tsebelis (1995, 294).
30. Cox and McCubbins (2001).

rectly on the design and redesign of the political architecture of countries around the globe. If Shepsle is correct and "discretion is the enemy of optimality, commitment its ally," institutional frameworks that concentrate decision-making power heavily are likely to give rise to chronic problems and welfare loss, with citizens, investors, and foreign actors facing an uncertain and potentially volatile policy environment. Conversely, if decisive and efficient governance is no less important than credible government, institutional frameworks that fragment power are also likely to give rise to serious costs, with decision makers failing to agree on timely policy responses to pressing social, economic, and political problems. Should we favor institutional frameworks that concentrate or fragment decision-making authority? Robust logics and formidable bodies of evidence have been assembled on both sides of this divide.

The second objective of this book is to propose a resolution to this puzzle. Juxtaposing these contending logics helps point the way to resolving the tension and developing a more satisfactory position. Let us take this step by step. On one fundamental issue there is implicit agreement across the literature: the more that power is institutionally fragmented among separate decision makers, the harder it is to reach an agreement to alter the policy status quo.[31] The fragmentation of power promotes policy stability; conversely, the concentration of power promotes policy flexibility. Figure 2.1 captures this essential logic in graphical form.

This much is uncontroversial. The disagreement, of course, is over which has more worrying implications: institutions that concentrate decision-making power or institutions that fragment decision-making power. Figure 2.2 highlights the contrasting logics by altering the terms of comparison and replacing the normatively neutral variable Potential for Policy Change on the vertical axis with the more analytically divisive variable that we can simply call Potential for Governance Problems. Commitments-type arguments see the concentration of decision making as the primary danger: the greater the concentration of decision-making power, the greater the risk of arbitrary action. This is characterized by the downward sloping line in

31. Tsebelis (1995) offers a formal analysis of this logic.

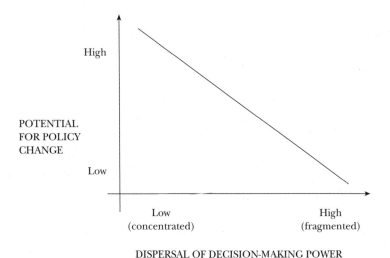

Figure 2.1 Dispersal of Decision-Making Power and Policy Change

this schema. By contrast, decisiveness-type arguments see fragmentation of power as the greatest enemy of good governance: the greater the dispersal of decision-making power, the greater the risk of paralysis. This is represented by the upward sloping line.

THE ARGUMENT

A better way to think about the relationship between institutions and governance is that either extreme on the horizontal axis is likely to be seriously problematic. A national political architecture that either severely centralizes or severely fragments decision making is likely to produce seriously problematic patterns of governance. The policy flexibility that is celebrated by those who underscore the importance of adaptable and decisive government behavior translates into policy volatility in its extreme form—a seriously problematic syndrome identified in the literature on credible commitments. But, conversely, the policy stability that is celebrated by those who underscore the importance of predictability and credible commitments

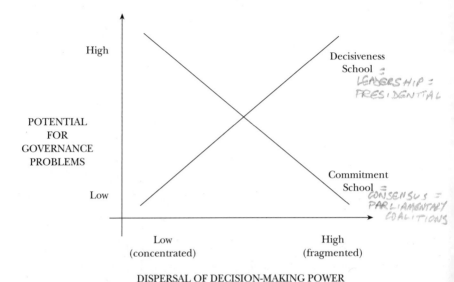

Figure 2.2 Dispersal of Decision-Making Power and Governance

translates into policy rigidity in its extreme form—a policy environment gripped by systemic inaction and paralysis suffers from a no less problematic policy syndrome. Either extreme policy syndrome—volatility or rigidity—undermines effective governance. The precise nature of the governance syndromes that lie at either end of the range differs, but both are seriously problematic. Herein lies the power concentration paradox.

Thus, on one hand, a country whose political framework fragments control over policy and disperses power widely among a range of political actors maximizes its ability to make policy commitments that are credible into the future. This is because, once made, achieving a new political consensus among all the various actors whose agreement is necessary is very difficult. As suggested by the literature introduced earlier, across the policy spectrum real benefits flow when citizens, investors, and international actors are confident about the future outlines of a country's policy environment and are able to plan accordingly. But the potential price of an institutional framework that maximizes commitment and stability is the likelihood that numerous other problems will accumulate and fester precisely because policy change—policy flexibility—is so difficult to achieve. The more power is fragmented, the greater the risk that policy rigidity will prevail. But, again, the converse is no less problematic. A country whose political system concentrates control over policy tightly in the hands of the national executive maximizes its ability to respond in a flexible and nimble fashion to both routine and unexpected policy problems. There are many advantages if government is able to tackle problems sooner rather than later, particularly those issues for which the cost of delay is high. But the potential price of an institutional framework that maximizes flexibility is the likelihood of volatility and even arbitrariness, with policy being subject to ready change or reversal and planning on the basis of expectations about the future policy environment becoming extremely difficult. The commitment school and the decisiveness school subliteratures both alert us to important truths, but neither directly captures the implications of their respective logics if carried to their extremes. It is this underlying trade-off that lies at the heart of the power concentration paradox: political architectures that maximize either policy stability or policy flexibility are likely to be simultaneously encouraging deeply problematic patterns of governance. Setting the issues up in this way has enabled me to extend the literature in new directions.

The key to resolving this puzzle is to recognize that despite their contrasting concerns about governance, commitments-type arguments and decisiveness-type arguments are causally linked by their institutional foundations. They are, in a sense, opposite sides of the same coin: flexibility versus stability or volatility versus rigidity. The common causal connection that produces the trade-off effect is the institutional configuration of power—the extent to which decision-making authority is dispersed. This only becomes clear when we juxtapose the two currents of theorizing as we have here. And this also points us toward a reasoned solution to our puzzle. In essence, there is a trade-off effect at work that has been little recognized by either current of scholarship. Political frameworks that severely concentrate decision-making power are indeed problematic, and introducing additional actors with institutionalized decision-making power does reduce the potential for volatility—but only up to a point, some unspecified point of inflexion, after which further dispersal of decision-making authority yields mounting problems of rigidity. Or, stated from the other side, political frameworks that severely fragment decision-making power are indeed problematic, and reducing the number of actors with institutionalized decision-making power does reduce the potential for rigidity problems—but only up to some unspecified point of inflexion, after which further narrowing of decision-making power yields mounting problems of volatility.

Another way of saying this is that the relationship between institutional configuration and governance is nonlinear. Rather than thinking in terms of a line that steadily rises or falls with the increasing dispersal of decision-making power, I contend that it is more helpful to think of this as a nonlinear relationship that passes through a minimum. That is, rather than as a straight line that rises and falls, we should think of this as a U-shaped curve. Figure 2.3 illustrates this alternative model.

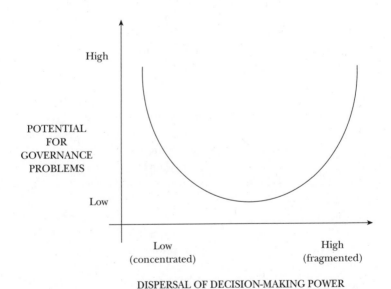

Figure 2.3 Decision-Making Power and Governance, the Power Concentration Paradox

Political reality is, of course, unlikely to be as neat or symmetrical as the perfectly U-shaped curve in figure 2.3; I have it stylized it this way for convenience and simplicity. Indeed, strictly speaking, in my theory, the only necessary condition is that the curve pass through a minimum—in other words, that it fall and then rise. Further, I have no theoretical basis for specifying a point of inflexion; indeed a more realistic way of thinking about this would be in terms of a zone of inflexion rather than a precise point. But these considerations are more refined than is necessary for the macrolevel claim that I am making—my core concern here is merely to argue that a U-shaped curve is a much better approximation of reality than either of the linear models implicit in the existing literature.

This argument, the power concentration paradox, captures some basic implications of the institutional configuration for governance and trade-offs that are inherent in this. It alerts us to the likelihood that basic governance problems are associated with both severely concentrated and severely fragmented institutional configurations. It tells us that managing policy change is likely to be increasingly problematic the further we move toward either extreme. I am not suggesting these are strictly necessary or inescapable outcomes. Institutional frameworks are enabling conditions—they set the organizational structure in which struggles over policy take place—but they are by no means the only factor that matters. There are, of course, many imaginable intervening variables[32] and we should not be surprised if there is some divergence from the predicted patterns. Nevertheless, on average, the logic of the power concentration paradox is likely to exert itself and show through.

Imagine a situation—mundane or dramatic—in which the policy status quo comes to be seen as unsatisfactory for some reason. How do different political frameworks respond to the challenge of forging an agreement for action to alter the policy status quo? A framework in which power is severely concentrated faces fewer obstacles to driving through a decision on policy reform, but, precisely because

32. To give just a few illustrations, the nature of the particular policy issue in question, the extent to which decision makers and their relevant constituencies are divided, the intensity of their preferences, and the timing of electoral cycles are all likely to make a difference.

of this, it is also likely to face increased risks that the reform measure itself will be susceptible to further adjustment and thus may not be trusted. Such a political framework does not necessarily exhibit policy volatility; the institutional configuration of power does not, of itself, compel this, but it does make it very much more possible. Thus, other things equal, this policy syndrome is much more likely to be encountered in countries whose political architecture is located toward the left-hand end of the range. And, conversely, a political framework in which decision-making authority is highly dispersed is not necessarily characterized by policy rigidity on every issue. But, again, all things being equal, the further we move to the right of the range, the greater the risk of immobilism.

What of countries whose political architecture is located away from the extremes and toward the center of the range? Should we expect them routinely to get things right by striking a happy balance? Again, not necessarily. Certainly we expect them to be less prone to either volatility or rigidity. They are less prone to volatility because their less-centralized political architecture has some provision for institutional checks on arbitrary executive action, and on the other hand they are less prone to rigidity because their less-fragmented political architecture makes the forging of agreement less difficult. But just as being located toward the extremes of the range is no guarantee that everything will go wrong, being located toward the center is no guarantee that everything will go right. This is in part because, as already indicated, intervening factors can make a difference. But more than this, being less susceptible to the basic problems of policy volatility or policy rigidity does not mean a polity is utterly free of governance problems. Keep in mind that we are operating at a fairly high level of aggregation and, as such, are focusing on the gross or macrolevel institutional picture. Although this enables us to bring the broad implications of institutional configuration for governance into clear perspective, it also means that we are likely to miss more specific implications that finer-grained analyses (which are the norm in institutionalist research) detect. Perhaps a simpler way of expressing this is to employ a physiological metaphor—the distinction between gross motor problems (say, problems in the movement of the arms) and fine motor problems (say, problems in the movement of the fingers).

A country whose political architecture is located toward the center of our range is unlikely to suffer gross motor problems, but this does not mean it is immune from fine motor problems.

Because my concern in this study is with the basic problems that are associated with the macro configuration of political institutions, my focus is primarily directed away from the center and toward the edges of the institutional range. This is the territory in which many developing countries are found, and it is also the territory in which the power concentration paradox speaks with greatest force. It is here that I make my primary contribution.

CHAPTER 3

Tools and Cases

In order to explore my argument about the implications of institutional configuration for governance I need an analytical measure
to enable me to compare diverse national political architectures. Although adjectives such as "concentrated" and "fragmented" are helpful for capturing stark differences in a general way, they are much less
helpful for differentiating shades of gray. We need to be clear about
what exactly is being compared and how it has been calibrated; comparative analysis can quickly become slippery once we get down to
the peculiarities of particular cases. Fortunately, theoretical work in
political science has produced a technique that is conducive to this
task—veto player analysis. In this chapter I outline this analytic technique and then put it to work by constructing initial profiles or characterizations of the political architecture of my four Southeast Asian
cases.

Veto Player Analysis

In simple terms, veto player analysis focuses on the interaction of a
country's constitutional structure and party framework to isolate actors who have the formal power to veto policy change. A "veto player"
is an individual or collective actor that has the institutionalized power
to defeat a proposed law by withholding formal approval—in short,
an actor in the legislative process with the institutionalized power to

37

say no. The more veto players there are, the more decision-making authority is dispersed. These fundamental ideas are quite straightforward and are scarcely new, a growing number of political scientists have employed them in order to make sense of basic differences in the way that governments function in diverse institutional settings. A number of variants on the core ideas have been employed since the early work of Ellen Immergut and then Evelyn Huber and colleagues,[1] but George Tsebelis has done more than anyone else to elaborate and formalize this method of analysis, and his approach is the point from which I start.[2]

The great virtue of veto player analysis is that it enables us to compare very different political architectures in a standardized way. Typically, comparative analysis has focused on particular classes of institutional variables for juxtaposition, such as parliamentary and presidential systems, bicameral and unicameral legislatures, two-party and multiparty systems, plurality and proportional electoral systems, and so on. By contrast, a veto player analysis allows us to embrace all of these within a single model. Tsebelis rightly celebrates its ability to deal with such institutionally disparate systems as Guatemala's unicameral multiparty presidentialism, U.S. bicameral two-party presidentialism, Greece's unicameral multiparty parliamentarism, and Australia's bicameral two-party parliamentarism.[3] This is very important given the diversity of the political frameworks in the Southeast Asian cases we are working with here. In addition to handling the full range of possible democratic configurations, as I show later, this framework can be readily extended to embrace semidemocracies in which the electoral playing field is not level and nondemocracies in which the electoral process is either nonexistent or heavily managed. In a sense, then, a veto player framework is an analytic tool that produces the equivalent of an X-ray image of a polity—highlighting the underlying institutional characteristics of the body politic. By focusing on only those actors who have an inalienable discretionary power to veto legislative change by withholding their approval, it al-

---

1. Immergut (1990, 1992); Huber, Ragin, and Stephens (1993). See also Maioni (1997); Birchfield and Crepaz (1998); Crepaz (1998); Shugart (2001).

2. Tsebelis (1995, 2000).

3. Tsebelis (2000, 442).

lows us to see past superficially distinctive or similar features among different national political architectures and systematically identify the extent to which decision-making power is concentrated or fragmented. If we wish, we can also introduce noninstitutional factors into the causal mix. Tsebelis and some others seek to do just this by also considering the effect of preferences and ideological distance among veto players.[4] But this is not my goal here; I stay strictly focused on the effect of institutional variables.

We begin with the unit of analysis—the veto player, the collective or individual actors whose agreement is necessary for legislation to pass. A collective veto player is a fixed group of people that routinely makes decisions on the basis of a majority vote. We meet collective veto players most often in legislatures. A cohesive political party serving in a parliamentary coalition government is an example of a collective veto player. An individual veto player is a single person—often called a president. The number of veto players varies across political systems and at any time reflects the interaction of a country's basic constitutional structure and its party system.

The easiest way to put flesh on these ideas to explicate the veto player analysis is to use concrete examples. Britain provides a convenient and familiar starting place. Although the British parliament formally has two chambers, in a veto player analysis the House of Lords is set aside because it has only the power to delay rather than actually veto legislation. The focus is thus on the Lower House. The party system is overwhelmingly dominated by two stable parties that routinely vote as cohesive blocs, so the larger of the two forms the government. In this framework, then, there is only one veto player: the governing party. The British framework is thus easily assessed—a single legislative chamber with veto power and a party system in which a single cohesive party controls the parliament.

If we work from this simple baseline, we can quickly see that the number of veto players increases with the introduction of constitu-

4. Although different from my own, this is an intriguing line of inquiry. I hope others will be motivated to extend it to developing-country contexts. In passing, I raise two issues that seem to complicate the task: the reality of log-rolling in a multidimensional policy world and the no less awkward reality that in many developing countries there is little ideological differentiation among parties.

tionally separate governmental structures, such as a second legislative chamber that has full veto power (rather than merely powers of review or delay) or a president who is endowed with legislative veto power. The United States provides a familiar example here, with legislative change requiring the separate consent of the House, the Senate, and the president. Similarly, we can quickly see the effect of the party system. In a given constitutional framework, the number of veto players increases with the introduction of multiple parties and coalition government. For example, if additional distinct parties were required to make up a majority in the British parliament—as routinely happens in a number of other parliamentary systems (e.g., Italy, Germany, and in recent times, Japan)—then the number of veto players would rise accordingly because policy change could only proceed if each party in the coalition agreed.

This much is fairly straightforward. An interesting and slightly more complicated variant arises with legislative assemblies in which, unlike the British House of Commons, individual parties are not strongly cohesive and do not routinely vote strictly along party lines as tightly disciplined units. The United States Congress provides a familiar example of this. In such cases, legislation is instead typically decided on the basis of ad hoc and shifting majorities that are put together issue by issue and routinely involve enlisting supporters regardless of party affiliation. If there is no stable partisan majority and the key voting decisions are, in effect, made by the chamber as a whole rather than by individual party caucuses, then it is appropriate to think of the chamber as a single veto player, no matter how many parties there may be within it. In short, where parties do not routinely vote cohesively, it makes little sense to treat them as distinct actors wielding veto power; it is more realistic to treat the whole chamber as the veto player. By contrast, where there is a stable legislative majority and the key votes routinely take place inside the individual parties rather than on the legislative floor, we treat each party within the governing coalition as an individual veto player.

Another interesting issue is how to handle cases in which the same party controls more than one legislative institution. For instance, sticking with the example of the United States, if the same party controls the presidency and both houses of Congress—as happened, for instance, in the first two years of the Clinton administration—does it still make sense to characterize this as a three veto player configuration? Given that the scope of debate is likely to be less than if there are opposing parties controlling the various legislative institutions, achieving agreement on policy change is likely to be easier. Accordingly, would it be a better representation of political reality to depict this as a case with just one veto player (the incumbent party) rather than three veto players? The answer is no. Although sharing the same party label increases the likelihood that politicians will agree, other institutional factors exert powerful countervailing influences: the nature of the constituency that politicians need to satisfy to win re-election (national vs. state vs. local district) and the timing of re-election (both term length and whether elections are concurrent).[5] Unless we can plausibly argue that different categories of politicians (in this case, a president, senators, and representatives) are primarily accountable to their parties rather than their respective sets of voters, it is more realistic to treat them as distinct because they are responding to different masters. Or, cast in principal-agent terms, unless we can argue that the party is the proximate principal for each of the categories of politicians, we should treat them as separate agents. In short, there are good theoretical reasons for believing that copartisanship is no guarantee that a president and a legislative assembly will agree. (And this, indeed, is what even a casual reading of U.S. history confirms.) Accordingly, except in very rare cases in which both constituency and electoral timing characteristics are congruent, we should treat institutionally separate veto players as distinct regardless of party label.

The essential elements of a veto player analysis are fairly straightforward—we identify those political actors that are endowed with institutional veto power over legislation and then tally the number of veto players, having regard for whether or not legislative chambers decide along strict party lines in a stable majority. These same basic principles apply even to nondemocratic political frameworks. The types of political rules and norms that matter in authoritarian polities may well be different from the ones that matter in democracies,

5. Shugart and Carey (1992); Lijphart (1984); Geddes (1994).

but this does not mean they are institution-free. This is a little explored subject, as noted earlier; however, the pioneering work of Shirk and Roeder on the communist frameworks in China and the Soviet Union provide powerful illustrations of this.[6] Except in very rare cases of pure dictatorships, the basic power relationships in authoritarian regimes are also structured and regularized by institutions—embodied in a formal national constitution, a set of internal party rules, or even an informal but routinized pact among members of a military junta.[7] Frequently, for instance, legislative assemblies that on paper have veto power in fact have no such power in any meaningful sense because other institutional arrangements ensure that they behave as mere rubber stamps for the person, party, or junta that controls the executive branch of the state. Or, again, to cast this in principal-agent terms, if it can be established that a de jure veto player (say, a legislative assembly) is indeed the agent of another (say, a president) then we should discount the former as a veto player. If the legislature is fundamentally beholden to the executive branch, then it enjoys no inalienable ability to withhold its consent and thus cannot be viewed as holding veto power. An example of this is Mexico up until the 1990s. Whether or not this applies in any given case is a matter requiring empirical investigation. But once a case has been specified empirically, the same basic analytical principles of the veto player framework can be employed.

There are many diverse permutations of constitutional structure and party system possible, that make the task of comparing the extent to which decision-making control over policy is dispersed or concentrated very tangled. A veto player framework gives us a simple and systematic gauge to do this. Although it is only a gross measure, it affords us some traction on the otherwise frustratingly slippery ground of comparing the extent of dispersal of decision-making power across countries with very diverse national political architectures.

6. Shirk (1992); Roeder (1993).

7. A good example of this is the initial junta established in Chile in 1973, under which Pinochet required the consent of the other services chiefs who made up the collective leadership of the junta. See Valenzuela (1991). I thank Matthew Shugart for drawing this to my attention.

42

VETO POWER IN THAILAND, THE PHILIPPINES, MALAYSIA, AND INDONESIA

Let us now turn from the abstract to the concrete. Armed with this analytical tool we can begin work on our four cases from Southeast Asia: Thailand, the Philippines, Malaysia, and Indonesia. This section specifies the extent to which decision-making power was dispersed in each country during the late 1990s, by focusing on actors with the institutional power to defeat policy change by withholding their formal consent. I sketch a quick profile of each case, drawing out the key features that are necessary to a veto player analysis.

Under the political framework in place in 1997, Thailand had a parliamentary system and, although there were two houses of parliament, the upper house only had powers of delay rather than of actual veto. Accordingly, only the House of Representatives carried veto power. However, because Thailand also had multiple weak parties— due in substantial measure to its electoral system[8]—control of the House was fragmented. With some ten to twelve parties represented in the parliament, a coalition government was inevitable, typically comprising six or more parties. So for our analysis, all parties in the coalition constituted veto players because they were all components of the majority necessary to pass legislation. If the prime minister and the rest of the cabinet attempted to override serious objections from a dissenting party to a proposed policy change, this would court the collapse of the coalition because the disaffected party could walk out of the coalition and, quite possibly, spawn a new parliamentary majority. Not surprisingly, governments were usually short-lived in this environment. In early 1997, there was a six-party coalition built around the New Aspiration Party and also including Chart Pattana, the Social Action Party, Prachakorn Thai, Seritham, and Muon Chon. We could, in fact, make a plausible argument that even a tally of six veto players understates the degree of dispersal of decision-making authority because some parties were only loose amalgams of

8. The pioneering work opening up a systematic institutional analysis of Thailand's party system and electoral system is from Hicken (1998, 1999, 2002).

coherent factions that could themselves threaten defection. For instance, the New Aspiration party of Prime Minister Chavalit Yongchaiyudh contained at least six main factions: the Sanoh (or Wang Nam Yen) faction, the Sukhavich faction, the Chin Chae faction, the Banong faction, the Pokin faction, and Chavalit's own faction. If our primary purpose were to develop a fine-grained image of Thai party politics, this would be an interesting line of inquiry. Indeed, just in terms of a narrow veto player analysis there are interesting issues that could be teased out, such as that a large faction inside a major party (say, the Sanoh faction) has more effective veto power than a small party (say, Muon Chon) in the overall governing coalition. But descending to this level of detail is unnecessary here given our more general purposes. The essential analytic point is captured by the already extraordinarily high number of veto players, the six parties in the cabinet. As we would expect given this high number, and as is confirmed by detailed accounts of politics and policy during this period, control over policy was dispersed to a quite extraordinary level.[9]

The framework of government in the Philippines was quite different both in terms of institutional design and the number of veto players. The Philippines was a presidential system of government with a bicameral legislature, in which both the House of Representatives and the Senate had full veto power on legislation. Like Thailand, the Philippines had a multiparty system, with roughly six incohesive parties gaining representation in the congress in the late 1990s. This necessitated the formation of multiparty coalitions in each chamber for legislation to be passed. Although the Philippines had a weak multiparty system like Thailand, this played out differently in terms of the distribution of veto power. The constitutional structure made a critical difference here. Unlike a parliamentary system, the political executive—the president—was elected separately and not beholden to the parties for tenure. The president did require the consent of a majority of each chamber for legislation to pass, but as long as a majority was achieved, its precise size and party composition did not matter. Because there was no stable majority of disciplined parties, the pres-

9. Hewison (1997); Pasuk and Baker (1998); Anusorn (1998); Hicken (1998).

ident constructed any coalition he or she could. In other words, the parties did not routinely decide their collective positions on legislative proposals and then act cohesively as voting blocs; instead, as in many other presidential systems, legislative majorities were constructed on an ad hoc basis. Accordingly, as per the earlier theoretical discussion, we should not view the individual parties as veto players but rather consider each of the legislative chambers as a single (collective) veto player.

In the Philippines, the fact that the presidency had a range of potent formal and informal discretionary powers at its disposal—high by comparison with many other presidential systems—facilitated the task of building legislative coalitions.[10] After elections, some legislators migrate to the party of the new president. Legislators remaining in the other parties had strong incentives to cooperate with the administration to pass priority legislation because of the president's on- and off-budget patronage powers.

During the period of interest to us, the Fidel Ramos administration, this became a finely oiled (if costly) machine.[11] Although the bargaining advantages at the disposal of the presidency could facilitate the advancement of the administration's policy agenda, as the experiences of both Ramos's immediate predecessor and successor made abundantly clear, the consent of congress could by no means be taken for granted. The net effect here is that whereas Thailand had a minimum of six veto players during the period in question, the Philippines had three: the president, the House, and the Senate.

Malaysia, in striking contrast to both Thailand and the Philippines, had a very much more centralized power structure. In common with Thailand, Malaysia had a parliamentary framework in which only the lower house of parliament has veto power. Malaysia also had a mul-

10. For an international comparison, see Shugart and Carey (1992, 156). Some observers worry that the presidency is too strong relative to the legislature. See, for instance, de Dios (1999), de Dios and Esfahani (n.d.) and Rocamora (1998). More generally, see the promising work by Yuko Kasuya (1999) and Gabriella Montinola (1999) that is casting new light on the linkage between the presidency and the weak party system in the Philippines.
11. Coronel (1998); Leones and Moraleda (1998).

tiparty system, but its characteristics differed in crucial ways, giving rise to a very different distribution of veto power. In broad terms, Malaysia can be thought of as having had a hegemonic party system, or a single-party-dominant system.[12] One umbrella party—the Barisan Nasional (or the Alliance, in its original incarnation)—had won every national election since 1955. Barisan was an ambiguous entity. It is often referred to as a coalition because it comprised a dozen separate parties, most notably, the giant elite Malay party, UMNO (United Malays National Organization). The various constituent member parties were organizationally separate and had distinct ethnically and regionally based memberships. Nevertheless, it is misleading to think of Barisan as a coalition because on the critical issues it actually behaved much more like a unitary actor or single party.[13] It was a very long-standing amalgam of parties with its own name and was itself formally registered as a party. More important, unlike the Thai pattern of volatile coalitions formed after elections by rival parties, Barisan's member parties divided up the electoral map among themselves before each election so as to avoid competing with one another. At election time, all members campaigned under the Barisan label rather than under those of the component parties, and it was the Barisan logo that appeared on the actual ballot. The absence of significant electoral or policy competition among member parties in Barisan[14] was in sharp contrast to the pattern in Thailand, where interparty competition within the governing coalition was just as fierce as it was with the opposition parties.

Viewed through the lens of a veto player framework, Malaysia had just one veto player, the politically cohesive actor that enjoyed a stable majority in the parliament—Barisan. Within Barisan, UMNO completely overshadowed the other dozen much smaller parties. Because

12. Jesudason (1999) offers a thoughtful interpretation of party politics using this lens.

13. Lijphart provides helpful criteria for assessing when it is appropriate to treat nominally distinct parties in a stable coalition as a single party (1999, 69–71). My thinking on this issue has benefited from discussions with Matthew Shugart.

14. A small and partial exception to this was the existence of some indirect and covert competition between the Malaysian Chinese Association (MCA) and Gerakan, two Chinese-based parties in Barisan. But as Gomez's (1998, 235) detailed account of Malaysia's party system indicates, this competition was at the margins.

UMNO was much larger than even the second largest party, unsurprisingly, UMNO dominated Barisan. Indeed, the smaller component parties depended on UMNO for financial resources to compete against the opposition parties at election time. Underlying and reinforcing UMNO's numerical preponderance within Barisan was the country's political history of deep ethnic cleavages. Although the smaller parties were represented in the cabinet, the great majority of positions, including those in all the key ministries—most notably the prime ministership—went to UMNO members. Analytically, it is helpful to think of Barisan as a set of nested delegation relationships, or concentric circles, in which members of the component parties delegated day-to-day decision-making power to their party leaders who sat in the cabinet, the leaders of the component parties sitting in the cabinet delegating to UMNO leaders and UMNO leaders delegating much to the prime minister. Any of these delegation relationships could be revoked—and the one from the UMNO party leaders to the prime minister periodically was. But for very many years it had suited the other constituent parties to continue to delegate the preponderance of authority to UMNO. In short, the smaller parties had long believed that they were better off inside this lopsided amalgam than outside. To defect from Barisan was to be consigned to the political wilderness—unlike Thailand's genuinely multiparty coalitions, in which a defecting party stood a good chance of being returned quickly to a new a coalition government in enhanced circumstances. The stability of the set of nested delegation relationships that made up Barisan derives from both the relative electoral strengths of the component parties and the politically delicate ethnic fabric. As was widely recognized, the effect of this stable arrangement was that the crucial political battles for leadership of the country were in practice fought within UMNO rather than within Barisan at large.[15] For most policy purposes—and certainly all those we are concerned with here—UMNO leaders spoke for Barisan as a whole. If UMNO leaders favored a policy change, it easily obtained cabinet approval and passed quickly into law because there were no

15. Gomez (1998); Milne and Mauzy (1999); Case (1996); Crouch (1996); Rais (1995).

other veto players to be reckoned with. Stated simply, Malaysia's framework functioned much more like Britain's disciplined two-party system (without the party turnover) than Thailand's volatile multiparty system. And compared to Britain, the position of the Malaysian executive had been strengthened further through creeping encroachments on democracy since the mid-1980s.

More centralized still was the unambiguously authoritarian case of Indonesia under Suharto. Indonesia's constitution specified both the president and the House of Representatives had veto power over legislation. Under the political framework developed during Suharto's long rule, however, the House was reduced to doing little more than rubber stamping legislation. This was not simply a result of informal intimidation or coercion. Under official statute, the executive branch had far-reaching formal control over all three political parties. Given a situation in which the president had—and used—the formal power to determine the number of parties, to have candidates declared ineligible for election, and to have sitting members recalled from the parliament, it makes little sense to think of the legislature as having veto power.[16] In effect, the power given to the legislature by the constitution was undermined by powers under separate statute enabling the president to control the parties. With the House having no effective veto power in the legislative process, there was only one veto player in this system: the president.

There is an interesting comparison with Malaysia here. During the period under review both had heavily centralized political frameworks. Both had only one veto player, but note the difference when that veto player is a single person as opposed to a collective actor. In formal terms, Barisan was the veto player in Malaysia; de facto this largely meant UMNO. In Malaysia's parliamentary framework, although Prime Minister Datuk Seri Mahathir Mohamad had far-reaching authority, he was nevertheless clearly constrained by the need to maintain support within Barisan and especially within UMNO. In In-

16. The removal of these laws was a key element of the democratic reform movement that followed Suharto's fall. For further details of the institutional framework under Suharto, see MacIntyre (1999b), Juoro (1998), and Surbakti (1999).

donesia's framework, Suharto's party had little independent life and imposed no policy constraints on him. Suharto was thus even less constrained than Mahathir with regard to control of the policy process. And, of course, in the background was the reality that coercion was a ready option for Suharto.

These thumbnail sketches of the institutional framework of government in the four countries highlight the degree of dispersal or concentration of control over the policy process by identifying the formal political actors with the institutionalized ability to block change. Comparing the diverse institutional frameworks of the four cases, Indonesia was the most centralized system (even more so than Malaysia, because the single veto player was an individual rather than a collective and because of the more authoritarian context); Malaysia also had a very centralized system featuring just a single veto player, followed by the Philippines with three veto players, and then by Thailand, much further along the range, with a very decentralized system of at least six veto players. Figure 3.1 provides a summary. These calibrations are only crude indicators, but they point to basic and highly consequential differences among the political systems.

Inevitably, abstract characterizations of what in reality are complex political systems beget questions. It may seem odd, for example, to equate some of these actors. Can a single party in a coalition in Thailand be meaningfully compared to the presidency in Indonesia under Suharto? Does it really make sense to treat the Philippine presidency and the House as if they were politically equivalent? My answer is yes. Remember that the veto player framework is being deployed here as an analytical lens to highlight a possible connection between institutions and governance across very diverse cases. My purpose is not to provide a fine-grained description of political reality; rather, it is to enable us to come to grips with an elusive but important feature of political life. It is certainly true that there are many respects in which not all the actors designated as veto players are equivalent. The Philippine presidency did often overshadow the House, and so on. But what all the actors identified here did have in common was the ability to kill policy change if they withheld their consent. In a multiple veto player situation, one veto player may in-

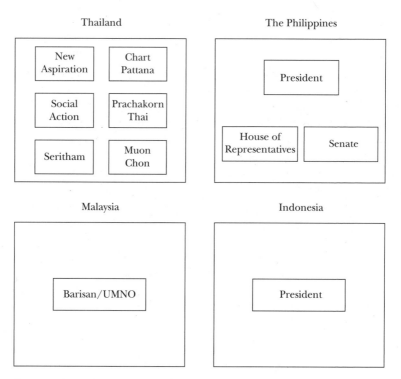

Figure 3.1 Veto Player Configurations at the Outset of the Economic Crisis, Early 1997.

deed have a greater ability to manipulate the incentives and calculations of the others, but, at a minimum, no veto player can take the cooperation of others for granted, precisely because of their inalienable and independent power to withhold consent.

Keep in mind also that the use of veto player is strictly delimited by definition. We are not referring simply to powerful people scattered throughout the state apparatus and society. In any polity there is, of course, a shifting array of individuals and groups who are able to mobilize resources—ranging from money to throngs of protestors—to block policy initiatives unwelcome to them. Although certainly remarkable and politically consequential, such actors do not constitute veto players. Such groups and individuals are the stuff of interest-based analyses. The starting point for an institutional analysis is that whatever the array of contending interests seeking policy satisfaction, they are all filtered or mediated through a political framework. Business tycoons and labor leaders alike work through veto players in order to achieve their objectives. In this sense, the national political architecture can be thought of as an intervening variable. My objective is to capture the differential effects of diverse institutional configurations.

With this in mind, how then do the X-ray images of the institutional bones of these four polities in 1997–98 tie in with the general theoretical claims I have made about the distribution of veto power and the likelihood of governance problems? In figure 3.2 each case is placed onto the U-shaped curve I proposed in chapter 2 on the basis of the distribution of veto power. Decision-making power in Thailand was severely dispersed across many veto players. This leads us to

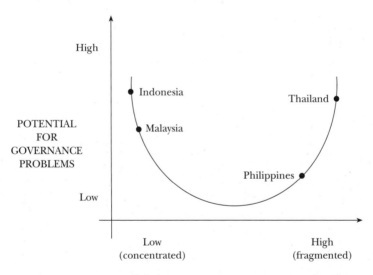

Figure 3.2 Decision-Making Power and Governance, the Four Case Studies in Early 1997.

expect that it would be susceptible to very serious problems of policy rigidity and places it high on the right arm of the curve. The political architecture of the Philippines produced significant—although not severe—dispersion of decision-making authority across three veto players (one individual and two collectives). This leads us to expect a significant although less extreme risk of policy rigidity and places the Philippines lower on the right arm of the curve. By contrast, Malaysia's configuration was quite concentrated, with just one (collective) veto player, which leads us to expect that it would be susceptible to problems of policy volatility and places it well up on the left arm of the curve. And Indonesia's decision-making power being severely concentrated in just one individual actor leads us to expect that it would be susceptible to very serious problems of policy volatility and places it high on the left arm of the curve.

This simple model has much to tell us about the causal connections between institutional configurations and governance. As we see in the next chapter, the generic policy syndromes expected under this model were indeed the ones exhibited in each case during the economic crisis of 1997–98.

CHAPTER 4

Political Architecture and Policy

This chapter provides empirical support for my claims about the significance of the configuration of political institutions for governance by tracing the policy responses of Thailand, the Philippines, Malaysia, and Indonesia to the Asian economic crisis of 1997–98. There are a number of reasons why the Asian economic crisis lends itself very well to this purpose. First, although any set of policy issues could serve as empirical grist for our analytical mill, the 1997–98 economic crisis is particularly useful because it provides an unusually consistent point of comparison for our four country cases—in its crucial early phases the crisis threw up remarkably similar challenges for each country at about the same time. To be sure, the economic circumstances of the four countries were not absolutely identical—reality is rarely that cooperative for social scientists—but they were all confronted with a dramatic loss of investor confidence in currency markets and then had to scramble to find ways of dealing with this problem. The second reason for using the regional economic crisis is that, as Peter Gourevitch observed some years ago, crisis episodes affecting multiple countries are especially useful in comparative analysis; they reveal starkly the bare bones of a polity.[1] When political systems are placed under severe strain, we can see much more clearly what they are made of and what they are capable of. Third, the economic crisis is, quite simply, the great story of the 1990s in

1. Gourevitch (1986, 9, 221, 240).

Asia. Not only does it carry a great deal of interest for its own sake, but this is the obvious policy case for anyone with an interest in Southeast Asia against which an argument about the systemic effect of political institutions on governance should be tested.

There is now a large and rich literature devoted to explaining the extraordinary economic upheaval in Asia in 1997–98. What began as an episode of currency instability in Thailand reverberated around the region, grew into a wider currency crisis, and then mutated into a much broader and deeper economic crisis. The sheer multi-dimensionality of the crisis has, inevitably, made it very difficult for observers to produce comprehensive accounts that capture the interactive effects of the domestic and international factors, factors that are variously economic, political, and social in nature. Not surprisingly, analysts have tended to focus on particular variables as key culprits, ranging from exchange rate mechanisms to corruption, from corporate governance to orthodox IMF policy prescriptions, from developments in China and Japan to global financial architecture, and from short-term debt to political legitimacy. Although the material and arguments I am working with certainly speak to the Asian crisis literature, my primary purpose here is not to contribute to it.[2] Rather, I draw evidence from this important and revealing episode to speak to wider debates about institutions and governance, and I use the behavior of these four states during the crisis to support a set of deductive arguments about how national political architecture affects policy form.

The essential economic outlines of the 1997–98 meltdown are familiar. Although the crisis ultimately produced severe economic turbulence for all countries in Asia with relatively open financial systems, clearly it did not afflict all such countries equally. This is plainly

2. For readers interested in the literature on the crisis itself, the following works are among the most useful. (I mention only the broader comparative studies here.) For early mainstream economic interpretations, see McLeod and Garnaut (1998) and Radelet and Sachs (1998). For mainstream political economy interpretations, see Pempel (1999), Haggard (2000), Noble and Ravenhill (2000), and Lukauskas and Rivera-Batiz (2001). For more skeptical and heterodox political economy interpretations, see Chang (2000), Jomo (1998c), Robison et al. (2000), and Wade and Veneroso (1998). And for World Bank and IMF perspectives, see International Monetary Fund (IMF 1999a, 1999b) and World Bank (1998b).

illustrated in our sample of four Southeast Asian cases. Although the Philippines suffered a major economic reversal—its annual rate of economic growth tumbled by six percentage points between 1996 and 1998—it suffered less than the others. During the same period, Indonesia's growth rate fell by twenty-two percentage points, Thailand's by fourteen points, and Malaysia's by fifteen points. A similar picture emerges if we look at other indicators.[3] The main point is clear: all were severely buffeted, but Thailand, Malaysia, and Indonesia were hit much harder than the Philippines.

There is much emphasis in the Asian crisis literature on what governments did and did not do in terms of pulling particular policy levers. But amid all the attention to this or that particular policy variable, there is little recognition of the broad patterns of policy management that become apparent if we draw back from the trees to consider the forest as a whole. The picture that emerges from the wider-angle perspective is striking. I show that, looking at the overall pattern of policy management during the crisis, Thailand presents a stark case of severe policy rigidity, whereas Malaysia and Indonesia present stark cases of severe policy volatility. Time and again, when there was a pressing need for Thailand to take decisive action, policy was paralyzed by disagreement inside the government. The net effect was that policy responses were typically severely delayed and diluted. In Malaysia and Indonesia the problem was the polar opposite; government took very quick and powerful steps in response to the unfolding crisis, but under the pressure policy became highly volatile, swinging from one direction to another. The net result was that the policy environment became severely confused and uncertain. In short, the three countries badly damaged by the crisis exhibited strong manifestations of the two counterpoised governance syndromes I have outlined: policy rigidity and policy volatility. Alone among our sample of cases, the Philippines did not exhibit strong symptoms of either extreme syndrome. To be sure, as elsewhere, Philippine decision makers struggled mightily to try to cope with the

3. Gross domestic investment (GDI) fell 7 percent in the Philippines, 41 percent in Indonesia, 37 percent in Malaysia, and 42 percent in Thailand. Capital inflows fell by 91 percent in the Philippines, 190 percent in Indonesia, 138 percent in Malaysia, and 158 percent in Thailand (MacIntyre 2001).

crisis, but, whatever other shortcomings they displayed, the overall pattern of policy management was at least an adequate compromise between the competing needs for decisive yet credible action. These striking divergences in the basic character of policy management are what interest me here. Elsewhere, I have taken the additional analytical step of arguing that we can see the diverging policy postures as an important causal factor in explaining the variance in the severity of investment reversals across the four countries in 1997–98.[4] My argument there is that, particularly in a time of regional economic instability, either of the extreme governance syndromes—severe policy volatility or severe policy rigidity—is likely to be very worrisome to investors who, on average, are looking for credible assurances that those elements of the economic policy environment requiring adjustment will be dealt with in a timely manner and that those elements requiring defense under pressure will remain constant. My primary concern here is not to link governance to economic outcomes but rather to track backward in the causal chain, highlighting the links between overall patterns of policy management and institutions. A careful examination of the empirical material reveals that lying behind these patterns of governance were precisely the institutional frameworks my theory leads us to expect. Lying behind Thailand's pattern of chronic policy rigidity was a political framework that fragmented power widely. Lying behind Malaysia's and Indonesia's pattern of policy volatility was a political framework that centralized power very tightly. And lying behind the Philippines's pattern of policy management—located between the two extreme syndromes—was a political framework located in from the polar extremes of political fragmentation and centralization.

This is my argument. What are the alternative arguments to which it can be compared? The short answer is that, unfortunately, there are no existing alternative analyses that are directly comparable. In the plethora of literature on the financial crisis—stretching from economics to political science to sociology—with multiple debates and analytic targets, nobody else has been primarily concerned with

4. MacIntyre (2001a). See also MacIntyre (1999a); Haggard and MacIntyre (2001).

identifying and explaining the broad pattern of policy management across these cases during the crisis period.

Yet the fact that no one has yet generated an alternative explanation for this pattern of empirical variance across the cases does not mean that there are no other imaginable interpretations. From which direction might we expect a reasoned alternative argument to come? Perhaps the most likely is an attempt to explain contrasting patterns of policy volatility and rigidity in terms of an interests-based story. We can imagine an argument focusing on the nature of the dominant coalition, identifying the specific constellation of interests being represented, and then attempting to probe the implications of this for the overall pattern of policy management.

It goes without saying that this is a common and powerful approach to comparative and international political analysis. And, indeed, it informs much of the single-country studies of Southeast Asia during the crisis.[5] But even if someone were to bring this analytical lens to bear in a systematic way across these four cases, it would not yield a satisfying explanation for the variance in the overall patterns of policy management.[6] All we would find is that the coalitional dynamics were broadly comparable across the four cases. In all four cases, the governments were built on mixed coalitions of capital (scattered across both export industries and nontraded manufacturing and services industries), farmers, and, in varying degrees, state officials. This does not come close to telling us why the policy environments in Malaysia and Indonesia were characterized by volatile swings, in Thailand by paralysis, and in the Philippines by steady and tolerably timely adjustment.

In saying this, I certainly do not mean to suggest that interests and other variables are irrelevant or that national political architecture is the only factor that matters in explaining the broad patterns of gov-

5. For important exemplars, see Pasuk and Baker (1998) and Robison et al. (2000).

6. A partial exception, which offers an interests-based account that does compare cases systematically, is an intriguing paper by John Sidel (1999a). But its purposes are quite different, being a macrohistorical comparison of late-nineteenth- and late-twentieth-century Southeast Asia, with particular attention to the position of Chinese entrepreneurs.

ernance across these cases. Indeed, as I make plain in due course, there are real limits to the analytical reach of institutionalist analysis. My purposes in this chapter are threefold. At an empirical level, I seek to show that there are clear and distinctive patterns in the overall management of policy by governments in these four cases. Second, at an analytical level, I seek to show that there are strong causal connections between these patterns of policy management and the underlying institutional configuration of each polity. And third, at a theoretical level, I suggest that these cases provide powerful illustrations of the power concentration paradox: institutional configurations that produce severe concentration or severe fragmentation of decision-making power carry distinct governance perils.

I treat the four cases in the order in which they were hit by currency instability—Thailand, the Philippines, Malaysia, and then Indonesia. In each case, I strive to provide enough detail to enable readers to appreciate the essential dynamics of the policy issues and struggles, while highlighting the overall policy pattern or posture that was emerging and linking this back to national political architecture. I do not provide the sort of exhaustive empirical account needed for a description of the full complexity of either the economic crisis or political life more generally in any of these countries. Rather, I draw out the overall character of policy management so that contrasting patterns of governance are highlighted and causal connections to underlying political architectures are exposed.

THAILAND

For Thailand, the economic crisis of 1997–98 did not suddenly begin with the fall of the baht on July 2, 1997. The decision to unpeg the country's currency and allow it to float, or rather fall, was the product of an amalgam of economic problems that had been growing for some time and that began to spin rapidly out of control from the beginning of 1997. Severe governance problems were a key underlying cause of this and of the subsequent failure to contain the economic crisis more effectively once it broke open. More specifically, the extreme fragmentation of veto power stemming from the institutional configuration of the political system was central to the inability of successive governments to tackle serious policy problems. In a situation that cried out for policy adjustment, government was simply unable to break out of the prevailing pattern of policy rigidity.

By late 1996, it was quite apparent that the Thai economy was in difficulty.[7] Overall economic growth was slowing (from 8.8 percent in 1995 to 5.5 percent for 1996). Exports in particular fell very sharply, after enjoying strong growth in previous years. The budgetary position, after having a surplus for nine successive years, was weakening markedly. More broadly, and of most concern, the country's overall balance-of-payments with the outside world had become very lopsided. With the deficit on the current account-to-GDP ratio sitting at a worryingly high 8 percent, Thailand's reliance on external funding to fuel its economy was reaching a decidedly unhealthy level. Compounding these macroeconomic problems, there were also serious problems in the financial sector. Thailand's banks, and particularly its finance companies, had grown very rapidly through the 1990s on the back of strong inflows of short-term foreign capital. Much of the new lending had gone into the property sector, however, and with the prolonged property boom finally failing by late 1996 serious doubts about the soundness of a number of finance companies emerged. Given these circumstances, it was not surprising that the country's pegged exchange rate became a target for speculative activity by the end of the year.[8]

There was no doubt that Thailand needed to adjust its economic policy settings to rekindle investor confidence and growth. Notwithstanding the seriousness of the situation, reform efforts were weak and inconclusive. With the government incapable of taking effective remedial action, Thailand's economic problems metastasized through the first half of 1997. The period leading up to the unpegging of the

7. For useful sources on the events leading up to and the management of the crisis in Thailand, see Nukul Commission Report (1998), Bhanupong (1998), Ammar (1997), Pasuk and Baker (1999), Warr (1998), Doner and Ramsay (1999), Lauridsen (1998), Hewison (2000), IMF (1999a, pt 2, chap. 4) and World Bank and National Economic and Social Development Board (1998).

8. Bhanupong (1998); Warr (1998); Ammar (1997).

currency can be thought of as a first phase, in which what should have been no more than a period of difficult economic adjustment was allowed to mutate into something much more serious. The collapse of the baht in July inaugurated a new phase in which efforts to contain the mounting crisis failed, and investors drew back even further, producing very grave economic dislocation.

Institutionally rooted policy rigidity was central to the mounting problems in Thailand and the subsequent failure to contain the situation more effectively once the baht began to depreciate. Much blame has been heaped on the government of Chavalit Yonchaiyudh, which had stewardship of the country through the critical months from December 1996 until November 1997 when the economy rapidly unraveled. But this government was no more beset by divisions, paralysis, or even corruption than any of the other short-lived elected governments that had preceded it. Indeed, at least to begin with, Chavalit's government looked stronger, more economically competent, and more promising than had its three elected predecessors. But like all its predecessors, Chavalit's government was profoundly constrained and soon broken by its severely fragmented power structure. As the institutional profile of Thailand in chapter 3 shows, decision-making power was so widely dispersed that there were no fewer than six veto players. For a prime minister to attempt to override serious opposition from a coalition partner was to invite defection and the possible collapse of the coalition. Although scarcely out of keeping with the experiences of previous governments, the titanic struggles in late 1996 over the allocation of portfolios and ensuing perquisites at the founding of Chavalit's new coalition government were revealing of what was to follow. Fierce struggles among and within parties dragged out the process of forming the cabinet over several weeks. Chavalit ultimately appointed no fewer than five deputy prime ministers to appease competing party interests. The lucrative Interior Ministry was carved up among several players, with three parties sharing the ministership and two deputy ministerships as well as the control of subagencies such as the police department. A small coalition party, Prachakorn Thai was given control of the traffic agency after it threatened to walk out of the fledgling coalition if it was denied its preferred plum. Very mindful of Thailand's accumulating economic problems, the Singapore press zeroed in on the key problem: "keeping a coalition of competing regional interests and ambitious party leaders contented is consuming more of his [Chavalit's] time than is warranted. It is time that Thailand cannot afford."[9]

Chavalit's government came to power after campaigning on a platform of tough new policy leadership to tackle the country's economic malaise. Chavalit installed Amnuay Virawan as finance minister and leader of the nonelected technocrats that he placed in key economic posts in the cabinet. This was intended to symbolize a new get tough approach to the country's economic drift, lifting core areas of policy management out of the hands of squabbling political parties and the shady dealings of the recent past. The approach harked back to the semidemocratic regime of General Prem Tinsulanond in the 1980s, when macroeconomic policy was managed by unelected technocrats.[10] But in the fully elected parliamentary framework of the mid-1990s, there was little scope for such a strategy. Coalition members could insist on full veto rights over matters of major concern to them.

The economic strategy that Finance Minister Amnuay began to outline in December 1996 was broadly orthodox in character and centered on hacking back government spending and tackling systemic problems in the financial sector. The government did not dare contemplate exchange rate adjustment for fear of the increased pressure this would place on the country's heavy foreign debt bill. Accordingly, the central bank simply attempted to hold off periodic speculative surges by spending down its reserves, clinging to the hope that policy adjustments on the macroeconomic and financial sector fronts would be enough to turn the economy around and prevent investor jitters from breaking the currency peg. In this situation, much was riding on the government's efforts to tighten the budget and shore up the financial sector. And these, in turn, depended on

9. "Chavalit Runs into Problems," *Straits Times,* 12 December 1996. For a wider discussion of party fights over the formation of the cabinet, see "Chavalit in Trouble with NAP Rejects," *The Nation,* 11 November 1996; "Quota Sparks Fight within Chart Pattana," *The Nation,* November 16 1996; "Snoh Pushes for 11 Seats in Cabinet," *The Nation,* 22 November 1996.

10. Doner and Laothamatas (1994).

securing the agreement of the various veto players represented in the cabinet.

On the fiscal front, Amnuay succeeded initially in obtaining cabinet approval for substantial spending cuts in an effort to reimpose some budgetary discipline and ease the current account pressures. A tighter fiscal stance also aimed at allowing the government to loosen monetary policy in an effort to help rekindle economic growth. But proposed big spending reductions in capital works programs for education, roadworks, and infrastructure projects created intense opposition within the cabinet because they threatened to eliminate prized pieces of legislative pork that were the essential lifeblood of party and electoral politics. The politics of this fiscal austerity drive were made worse as a slowing economy produced smaller-than-expected tax yields, forcing the finance minister to seek still further spending cuts in pursuit of the original goal of confidence-building.[11] And the more the cabinet dragged its heels, the bigger the problem became. Indeed, slow and half-hearted cuts could be worse than no cuts because they were unlikely to impress the markets and yet still exacted some contractionary toll. And as serious tax shortfalls emerged, the government was forced to seek still further cuts. As one parliamentarian put it in late January, "The government needs to have courage, a clear policy and quick decision-making or else the targets of saving and economic stability will not materialize."[12] Notwithstanding the premium on timely and decisive action, this proved all but impossible as one party after another—most notably New Aspiration (the prime minister's own party), Social Action, and Chart Pattana—dug in their heels over cuts to their particular bailiwicks. Faced with the prospect of defections from the coalition, Chavalit's only option was to accept delay.[13] After weeks of cabinet procrastination—and then, only on the eve of a visit by Moody's credit rating agency and an impending yankee bond issue—Amnuay

11. "Budget Cut to Be Doubled to Restore Confidence," *Bangkok Post,* 31 January 1997.

12. "Revenue Shortfall Predicted: State Spending Must Be Trimmed Further," *Bangkok Post,* 30 January 1997.

13. See, for instance, "Two Problems Threaten to Blow up Coalition," *The Nation,* 18 February 1997; "Interior Uproar over Cuts Predicted," *The Nation,* 4 March 1997.

succeeded in securing an in-principle endorsement for more extensive cuts.[14] But this failed to have the desired confidence-building effect, in part because of the protracted process. When continued economic deterioration soon forced Amnuay to return to his cabinet colleagues seeking approval for still more spending cuts, opposition to his proposals hardened within the coalition, with one party digging in its heels in June over an additional excise increase. Forced to choose between the survival of his coalition and his technocratic finance minister's reforms, Chavalit, not surprisingly, opted for the former, causing the dispirited Amnuay to resign.[15] Coalition politics had claimed an early ministerial scalp and struck a serious blow to the government's standing in the eyes of the markets. There was general agreement on the need for fiscal adjustment, but the existence of so many veto players made its achievement extremely difficult.

The underlying political malady was not peculiar to budgetary policy and politics. If we turn our attention to the other key policy front on which the government was fighting to shore up confidence—the financial sector—we see the same underlying political dynamics at work. It was widely suspected that there were problems in the financial sector, particularly among the country's ninety-one finance companies. Previous governments had conspicuously failed to tackle the emerging problems in the financial sector. The initial signals the new government projected suggested that it might reverse this trend. But as it was put to the test in 1997, here too it proved no more capable of decisive remedial action.

By February 1997 the situation in the financial sector was beginning to unravel with the first default on a foreign loan, followed by an announcement that the country's largest finance company was seeking a merger to avoid collapse. In the face of widespread fears of an impending financial implosion and the beginnings of hurried depositor withdrawals, all attention focused on the government's re-

14. "Cabinet Forces Bt106 Bn in Cuts on Public Sector," *The Nation,* 12 March 1997.

15. "PM Fails to Settle Cabinet Conflict," *Bangkok Post,* 17 June 1997; "The Nation Fares a Poor Second to Politics and Personal Ambition," *Bangkok Post,* 20 June 1997. Economist Intelligence Unit, Thailand, 1st Quarter 1997, pp. 15–16; 2nd Quarter 1997, pp. 16–17; 3rd Quarter 1997, p. 17.

sponse to the situation. In a joint move on March 3, Finance Minister Amnuay and Rerngchai Marakanond, the central bank governor, suspended trading of financial shares and announced on national television a series of emergency measures designed to reassure nervous markets. The two key elements of the policy intervention were a requirement that all banks and finance companies make much stronger provisions for bad debt and an announcement that ten of the weakest finance companies would have to raise their capital base within sixty days.

These measures did little to reassure markets, and when trading resumed financial shares fell heavily amid reports of a rush to withdraw funds. Underlying continuing market nervousness were doubts about the government's ability to follow through with its proclaimed restructuring plans. Was the rest of the government really onboard? Concerns of this sort proved well founded. No sooner had Amnuay and Rerngchai targeted the ten ailing finance companies in their get tough campaign than determined opposition emerged from within the government. Several senior members of the government had interests in some of the ten targeted institutions and were easily able to use their position within the coalition to veto the enaction of the tough measures outlined by Amnuay and Rerngchai. Further, not only was no action taken against the ten finance companies, the central bank had to pump in large sums of new capital in order to keep them afloat in the face of runs by panicked investors.[16]

This was a critical juncture in the development of the crisis in Thailand. There was a clear and pressing need for effective government action, with widespread concern among Thai and foreign investors about the scale of the bad-debt problem in the financial sector. At the same time the baht was coming under mounting pressure, with currency market players sensing exchange rate vulnerability. Amnuay and Rerngchai did not dare pursue the strict path favored by financial hawks: forcing shareholders to accept big losses by allowing ailing institutions to fail or permitting foreign investors to take a controlling

16. "Implicated Politicians," *The Nation,* 18 April 1997; "Many Affected by Financial Scandal," *The Nation,* 13 March 1997; "Sanoh Dangles Promises to Appease Sukavich Faction: Party to Keep Paying Rebels B100,000 Each," *Bangkok Post,* 19 August 1997; Pasuk and Baker (1998, 105–10).

stake in these institutions. However, even the intermediate path they opted for—lifting capital adequacy provisions and singling out the weakest institutions for immediate attention—proved unattainable. These initiatives failed not because they were blocked by popular outcry or parliamentary opposition but because they were vetoed by members of the ruling coalition. Rather than risk the collapse of his new government as his predecessors had, Chavalit preferred to gamble on further compromise and delaying measures.

The finance minister's inability to follow through on even the moderate plans he had outlined had a very corrosive effect on investors. The government not only failed to deliver the reform plans that the market was apparently calling for, it failed to deliver the reforms it itself had publicly announced. As one minister close to Chavalit lamented, "To solve economic problems we cannot simply announce economic measures, we have to follow up on their progress."[17] But strong opposition from just one member of the coalition prevented ministers from following up on their announced plans. In addition to undermining the government's standing in the eyes of the market, the compromising and delaying measures that ultimately emerged only made matters worse. A side effect of not closing the ten finance companies and instead injecting them with large-scale emergency funding was the rapid expansion in the money supply (by 10 percent in the month of June alone). This served only to sharpen the fundamental contradiction in the government's overall macroeconomic position. At the same time that it was pumping money into the insolvent finance companies to keep them afloat, the central bank was also spending down reserves to prop up the exchange rate. As was increasingly recognized by markets, this was not a sustainable strategy. In mid-May the baht suffered its heaviest assault, but by this time it was no longer just big Thai companies and foreign investors that were betting against the baht, middle-class Thais were also increasingly moving to dollars.[18]

With a diverse coalition and all parties having incurred massive debts in order to win office, there was little prospect of the cabinet

17. "Thailand: Rudderless," *Far Eastern Economic Review,* 29 May 1997, 14–15.
18. Ammar (1997, 2); Fane and McLeod (1999, 4).

agreeing to take tough measures that might hurt the economic interests of ministers or their supporters. It is, of course, entirely normal, particularly during times of difficulty, for a range of distressed economic interests threatened by proposed government actions to seek special relief; this is true in all polities. But, in a polity that fragments veto power very widely—where there are many diverse political actors with the power to block unwelcome measures—the scope for resisting change is very great. Even if a majority were in favor of taking reform action, a minority prepared to play hardball could veto the action by threatening to walk out of the coalition.

By June 1997, Finance Minister Amnuay was gone. There was a rapid turnover in personnel in key government positions as the year progressed, but the same basic policy dynamic continued inexorably to exert itself, paving the way for the country's slide into further economic disarray. As the chief economist for Deutsche Morgan Grenfell ruefully observed of Amnuay's fall, "The problem is not with Dr. Amnuay, but with the entire cabinet. No matter who succeeds him, he will be subject to the same pressures. . . ."[19] And indeed, the man eventually found to succeed Amnuay, Thanong Bidaya, fared little better. Thanong began by trying to move decisively and seize the initiative. On June 27, he announced the suspension of sixteen finance companies (including seven of the original ten), giving them thirty days to implement merger plans. At the same time, however, the central bank was nearing the end of its rope in its doomed attempt to prop up the baht through currency-market intervention. With its reserves effectively exhausted, on July 2 the central bank announced that the baht was being cut loose. In a move that quickly reverberated around the region, the baht immediately fell very sharply, depreciating by 17 percent.

Thanong's priority remained the struggle to avoid widespread collapse in the financial sector. But although he had won approval for the announcement of the suspension of the finance companies, the leaders of one coalition member, Chart Pattana, were able to block the implementation of the initiative. Not only did Chart Pattana succeed in preventing the closure or forced merger of the sixteen fi-

19. "Amnuay to Resign after Tax Rise Blow," *Bangkok Post,* 18 June 1997, 1, 3.

nance companies, it also managed to persuade the central bank to continue injecting large sums of capital. In late July, in the context of negotiations with the IMF to obtain a rescue package, it was revealed that emergency loans to the sixteen finance companies now totaled a staggering Bt430 billion. (This figure exceeded the actual capital funds of the finance companies themselves and corresponded to approximately 10 percent of GDP.) The government naturally sought to downplay its own direct involvement in this scandal and instead forced the resignation of the recently appointed central bank governor, Rerngchai.[20]

A week later, on August 5, in an effort to regain the initiative and to satisfy IMF demands for commitment to policy reform, Thanong announced that a further forty-two finance companies would be suspended because of the scale of their loan problems and imminent insolvency. A total of fifty-eight, or two-thirds of the country's finance companies, had now been suspended. As were the earlier sixteen, this batch was given a short period in which to meet the tough new capital adequacy rules, merge with a stronger institution, or go out of business.[21] Again, however, there were questions about whether the government would be able to deliver on these pronouncements, with persistent rumors of irregularities in the committee established to vet the rescue plans of the suspended finance companies. In an effort to rectify this problem, a new committee leader was appointed, Amaret Sila-on, the respected head of the Thai Stock Exchange.[22]

But as one section of the government was trying to overhaul the financial sector, others were moving in precisely the opposite direction. The pattern was familiar, and the prime minister was powerless to resolve the tension. As one senior Thai business commentator put it at the time, "What investors are worried about is political interference in the implementation of the measures, something that we have

20. "Govt Allegedly Blames Central Bank Governors," *Bangkok Post,* 14 August 1997.
21. The government also announced that all depositors would be protected and that deposit insurance would be set up for the remaining healthy institutions. But, as before, this failed to prevent a three-day bank run.
22. "Amaret Tipped to Head Merger Screening Body," *Bangkok Post,* 26 August 1997.

seen over the past two to three years, where previous attempts to address the problems have failed because of political interference."[23] With the deadline for deciding the fate of the suspended finance companies looming, the politics intensified. In early October, the Association of Finance Companies vigorously courted Prime Minister Chavalit as well as Chatichai Choonhavan, a Chart Pattana leader, seeking a relaxation of the criteria for their rehabilitation. The IMF responded by publicly expressing concern that the independence of Amaret's screening committee not be undermined, but this had little effect. A week later, Amaret resigned after only a short tenure, declaring that he was being undercut by forces in the government.[24] Yet again policy adjustment was stifled.

Further concessions were soon made to the agenda Chart Pattana was pushing. At the same time that he announced the creation of two new independent agencies to handle the evaluation and processing of the targeted institutions, Thanong also revealed that the deadline for their restructuring would now be extended (without setting a new date) and that loans provided earlier to the ailing finance companies by the central bank could be treated as equity—thus opening the probability that the public resources injected into these companies would never be recovered.[25] And in another rearguard move, Chart Pattana succeeded in holding up the approval by the cabinet of the plans for the two new agencies announced by Thanong until text was inserted into the decrees specifically reversing their independence from the government.[26]

By this stage, however, the political situation was in a state of collapse. On October 19, Thanong resigned as finance minister over the vetoing of a gasoline tax a mere three days after it had been announced as part of the government's very long-awaited policy response to the IMF bailout. And in the wake of maneuvering in preparation for the formation of an expected new government led

23. "Financial Reform Package," *Bangkok Post,* 15 October 1997, Business section.
24. "A Big Blow to the Government: Amaret Quits Financial Rescue Team," *Bangkok Post,* 12 October 1997.
25. "Latest Finance Company Move Criticized by Analysts," *The Nation,* 12 October 1997.
26. Economist Intelligence Unit, Thailand, 1998, p. 13.

by Chart Pattana and impending defections in Chavalit's own party, the crippled prime minister announced his own resignation on November 3.

Thailand had fallen into deep trouble. Investor confidence had been routed: the exchange rate had fallen continuously (losing 25 percent of its value by the time of Chavalit's fall), capital was flowing out of the country rapidly, and lending had dried up. Central to this was the chronic inability of government to deliver necessary policy adjustments. Like its predecessors, Chavalit's government had become stymied by internal coalitional disagreement. But given an institutional framework with so many veto players, this was scarcely surprising. This striking inability to launch effective reform measures sent powerful signals to the investment community; the government—any government operating under this institutional framework—was incapable of delivering desperately needed reform. The new government built around Chuan Leekpai's Democrat Party— and including some parties from Chavalit's government—soon fell into this same familiar pattern. There was a short period from the end of 1997 through early 1998 when the new government was able to make some headway as a result of both an initial honeymoon effort and severe IMF conditionality, but before long the inexorable logic embedded in the country's political framework reasserted itself and the pace and scope of policy adjustment wound down as usual. The extreme fragmentation of veto power that was institutionalized in the Thai political system generated severe and chronic policy rigidity. In Thailand, then, we can see a clear connection between institutions and the quality of governance.

THE PHILIPPINES

The Philippines presents an important contrast with Thailand, both in terms of its national political architecture and the prevailing pattern of governance. As shown in chapter 3, the institutional framework in the Philippines provided for a significant dispersal of decision-making power across three veto players—the president, the House, and the Senate. (Recall that, viewed through the analytic lens of a veto player framework, we treat the House and Senate as single collective actors because neither routinely decided policy on the basis of stable party voting.) The existence of multiple veto players leads us to expect that rapid policy change would be difficult. But the extent of the dispersal of decision-making authority here was much less extreme than in Thailand. The Philippines had an intermediate configuration—a configuration that was neither severely fragmented nor severely centralized. This leads us to expect that its characteristic pattern of governance would be somewhere between the extremes of policy rigidity and policy volatility; we expect to find that policy change in the Philippines was difficult, but not to the point of rigidity. This turns out to be a remarkably good guide to the overall response of the Philippines to the unfolding 1997–98 economic crisis.

The crisis struck the Philippines in the final twelve months of Fidel Ramos's term as president, when his authority was declining both because of his lame-duck status and because of the criticism brought down on him by the futile attempt of his supporters to circumvent his constitutional term limit. In spite of this, when important policy adjustments were needed in the face of the mounting economic crisis and when the full weight of the presidency was brought to bear on the task of facilitating agreement among all actors wielding veto power, the system worked satisfactorily. Certainly there was protracted debate within the House and the Senate as both chambers struggled to decide their collective positions on complex matters such as urgent tax reform. And there was further struggle as the two chambers negotiated to resolve the differences between their respective positions on the substance of policy adjustment. And, certainly, there was also all the usual back-corridor wheeling and dealing as the president sought to facilitate a consensus that was both timely and close to his own substantive position. In short, all the usual practices that provide the grist for the mills of Philippine editorial writers and that distress many observers of Philippine politics were on display—the haggling, the stalling, the self-serving behavior, the threats, and the dubious inducements. The much more remarkable point, however, is that, unlike in the Thai situation, this was done within a framework of government that was functional—perhaps not optimal, but at least functional. The overall pattern of policy management was subject to neither the problems of severe policy rigidity associated with a wide dispersal of veto power (as in the Thai case) nor the problems of severe policy volatility (as in the Malaysian and Indonesian cases, discussed later). We can thus observe an example of a political framework with a moderate distribution of veto power coping with a crisis situation.

A subsidiary point that also feeds into our overall interest with political institutions and governance is the difference between the scope for executive action in the Philippine system as opposed to the Thai system. A number of policy adjustments relevant to the economic crisis—most obviously, exchange rate and monetary policy issues—were typically the province of executive agencies or central banks and thus did not directly involve the legislature. That is, the legislature had in effect previously delegated the management of these issues to such agencies. This proved advantageous in the Philippines with its presidential framework, but of no advantage in Thailand with its multiparty parliamentary coalition government. Presidentialism implies that executive decision-making authority is ultimately concentrated in a single individual. In Thailand however, executive authority was much more fraught because the executive—the cabinet—was a collective body containing all the veto players.

In the time leading up to the crisis, the Philippine economy was not slowing (unlike Thailand), its export sector was not sagging, and it had not built up heavy short-term foreign debt in the private sector.[27] In part, this was because the growth spurt in the Philippines was much more recent than elsewhere and the Philippines had therefore only reentered international capital markets in 1993. From this perspective, as others have noted, the Philippines did indeed seem a less likely candidate than Thailand for a dramatic investment reversal.[28] Nevertheless, the economy was by no means without problems. There were real difficulties in some macroeconomic areas: persistently low savings and persistently high public debt paired with rapid

27. More detailed accounts of various aspects of the Philippine experience through the crisis can be found in Hutchcroft (1999), Mijares (1999), Alburo (1998), Intal et al. (1998), Sicat (1998), Jurado (1998), Lim (1998), Montes (1999), and IMF (1999a, pt. 2, chap. 5).
28. Hutchcroft (1999); Sicat (1998).

credit growth. As a number of economists have pointed out, there were emerging questions of the competitiveness of Philippine industries, and in the period immediately prior to the onset of the crisis there were unhealthy trends emerging in the financial sector, with the proportion of foreign borrowing and the proportion of lending on real estate and other nontradables beginning to rise quickly.[29]

How did policy makers in the Philippines respond to the crisis? Although there were certainly political obstacles to adjustment, we do not see the crippling pattern of systemic policy rigidity exhibited by Thailand. After a brief and costly effort to defend the currency, on July 11, 1997, the peso was allowed to depreciate sharply. From this point, compared to what other countries in the region did, the Philippines followed a reasonably consistent orthodox approach. The key elements were adjusting monetary policy, enhancing bank regulation, and tightening fiscal policy. All three were important. The country's institutional framework facilitated a relatively smooth policy adjustment in the first two, but rendered the politics of fiscal management much more complex. Even here, however, despite messiness and delay, a tolerably timely and coherent outcome was achieved. The Philippines exhibited neither of the extreme policy syndromes, and this is consistent with the distribution of veto authority inherent in its institutional framework.

On the monetary front, the central bank, Bangko Sentral ng Pilipinas (BSP) worked closely with the government to drain liquidity from financial markets through the second half of 1997. A number of tools were used: open market operations, ratcheting up the liquidity reserve requirements and loan-loss provisions, and pushing up BSP's own overnight rates and occasionally even closing BSP's overnight window. With the exception of urgent attempts to force rates sharply higher for short periods (in the face of a new wave of currency uncertainty), the rise in rates was fairly gentle. The peso reached its low point in the first week of January 1998. From roughly the beginning of 1998, BSP moved steadily to ease rates as pressure on the peso seemed to be subsiding and the alternate danger of keeping monetary policy too tight came increasingly apparent.

29. De Dios et al. (1997); Intal et al. (1998).

By comparison with Thailand, the policy rhetoric and policy action of the Philippine government were much more closely correlated. The configuration of veto power meant that there were far fewer obstacles to delivering on declared policy goals. Through the first phase of the crisis in the second and third quarters of 1997, BSP (working in close consultation with the administration) sent steady signals about its intentions to keep monetary policy tight, and then, when circumstances appeared to warrant an easing in early 1998, it moved steadily to bring this about. This was not a frictionless process; indeed, lowering interest rates proved to be more difficult than raising them. A range of inducements, together with the threats from Gabriel Singson, the BSP governor, through the first quarter of 1998 to reintroduce lending rate controls and allow in more foreign competitors if banks failed to narrow their lending spreads, was needed before lending rates subsided.[30] Nevertheless, compared to what we observe elsewhere, BSP moved in a coherent and steady fashion. And even more important, it was not undercut by contradictory signals from other branches of the administration.

Enhanced prudential and oversight arrangements for the banking sector were the second key policy focus. The Philippines had undergone a long-running reform process in the banking sector in the wake of a major financial crisis in the early 1980s.[31] In the period leading up to the outbreak of the financial crisis in 1997, BSP had moved preemptively to limit bank exposure to the property sector and increase cover against foreign exchange volatility. Once the crisis erupted, it took additional steps in this direction: lending to the property sector was further tightened, the classification and reporting requirements of nonperforming loans were tightened, a hedging facility (nondeliverable forward contracts) to limit foreign exchange risk was brought in, minimum capitalization and provisioning for bad-loan requirements were strengthened, and stricter eligibility rules for investors in banks and bank presidents were introduced.[32]
Institutionally, these measures were relatively easy to introduce.

---

30. Economist Intelligence Unit, the Philippines, 2nd Quarter 1998, p. 18.
31. Hutchcroft (1998, chaps. 8–9); Intal et al. (1998, 146–48).
32. Singson (1998b).

On issues that fell within the purview of the specific powers delegated to it by the legislature (and underwritten by the constitution), BSP could act executively to affect regulatory change in the banking sector. In these areas, then, BSP, in coordination with the administration, acted in a timely fashion to introduce measures to reduce the risk of bank failure and thereby boost wider investment confidence in the stability of the Philippine economy. As a result, bank failures were minimal in the Philippines. Several minor institutions closed, but their combined deposits amounted to barely .25 percent of total deposits in the banking system.[33]

The third key policy front—fiscal management—was no less important, but much more complex politically. The fiscal picture deteriorated rapidly over the course of 1997; a surplus of P6.26 billion had been achieved in 1996 and the original target for 1997 was P12.96 billion, which in actuality shriveled to just P1.56 billion. The outlook for 1998 was bleaker, not least because of the government's rapidly increasing interest obligations arising from the intensified open-market monetary policy operations. The deteriorating fiscal situation quickly became a concern, with the government struggling to prevent this from exacerbating investor nervousness and driving the currency down further. Its response was broadly consistent with its monetary policy operations: it took a stiff orthodox position, persevering with the conservative fiscal posture assumed in the previous few years. But whereas on monetary and bank supervisory issues the administration, in conjunction with the central bank, enjoyed a high degree of operational autonomy, in the fiscal arena the political situation was much more complex. Institutional arrangements were central to this—on some important issues the administration's plans were confounded by other branches of government, whereas on others the path to policy action was much clearer. The critical difference lay in the details of the veto structure.

For example, the administration could cut expenditure with relative ease. Although the president needed congressional consent to spend more than the approved budget, there were no obstacles to his

<hr />

33. Singson (1998a).

spending less. Ramos could thus unilaterally order a 25 percent across-the-board cut in all nonpersonnel departmental spending. Contrast this with the Thai situation, in which the multiparty collective executive structure of the government caused finance minister Amnuay (and his successors) to have to fight hard against all the parties in the cabinet for every budget adjustment.

Serious problems did arise for Ramos, however, in two fiscally related policy areas that came to assume bellwether significance in the context of the wider economic nervousness: income tax and oil deregulation. Both policy reforms were held up by congressional opposition. Both had powerful budgetary implications and thus fed directly into the ability of the administration to reassure nervous markets about the exchange rate. And both were formal requirements for the Philippines to graduate from the existing IMF Extended Fund Facility (EFF). More important, as the regional economic crisis intensified the IMF made the satisfactory legislative completion of these reforms a condition for new emergency assistance (standby credit facilities) to assist the central bank's efforts to stabilize the currency market.

Reforming the income tax laws had been a long-running political battle in the Philippines. A comprehensive reform of tax laws was central to the EFF agreement that the Ramos administration had established with the IMF in 1994. Income tax was the last remaining component, having been the subject of protracted debate within the congress and between the congress and the administration. By early 1997, pressure for a resolution was mounting because the EFF was scheduled to expire at the end of June. But with elections looming in 1998, legislators were naturally keen to champion the cause of higher tax-free thresholds against the more austere fiscal plans of the government. Despite presidential pleas for cooperation, one target date after another passed, with the administration being forced to request repeated extensions of the EFF deadline. Even greater urgency was injected into the whole matter as the peso tumbled and the regional financial crisis built up a head of steam in the second half of 1997. The reform bill had been tied up first in negotiations inside both the House and the Senate and then in a bicameral conference committee to reconcile differences between the respective drafts by the two chambers.[34] Issues such as tax exemptions were inherently sensitive electorally, directly affecting both the general public and particular large businesses. Inevitably, this made for difficult and complex politics. The administration's position had, of course, been crafted with the requirements of the IMF in mind. The Senate's draft bill was much closer to the administration's position than was the House's. Accordingly, the most intense political negotiations were focused on the House. Ultimately the president had to become actively involved in working with House Speaker Jose de Venecia to persuade the House to yield to the Senate version. De Venecia was legendary for his ability to craft majorities on the basis of political and economic side-payments to legislators. His services to the president at this point were indispensable and presumably played into Ramos's agreeing to nominate de Venecia as his chosen successor for the 2000 presidential election.[35] A legislative deal was finally reached on December 8 and quickly signed into law by Ramos. Although much delayed, the final outcome satisfied the political needs of the three veto players and the IMF's core economic requirements for a more effective tax system and increased revenue.[36] The outcome was late, but not intolerably late, and contributed directly to the government's ability to present a credible policy posture to nervous markets.

We see a very similar pattern in the other fiscal-related policy reform that tied into the government's overall policy stance in the face of the crisis—oil deregulation. Deregulation of the oil sector may seem an unlikely ingredient in the solution to a financial crisis, but it played directly to the soundness of the government's fiscal posture, its access to IMF support, and, in powerful symbolic fashion, the country's reputation with investors for effective governance. Just as the protracted income tax saga was coming to an end, oil deregula-

34. "Congress Fails to Resolve Debate on Tax Exemptions," *Business World* (Manila), 17 October 1997; "The Comprehensive Tax Reform Program," *Business World* (Manila), 17 October 1997.

35. "Ramos Threatens to Wield Big Stick," *Philippine Daily Inquirer,* 23 November 1997; "Power, Pork, Presidency, and Joe de V," *Manila Times,* 10 December 1997; Magno (1998, 207).

36. Economist Intelligence Unit, the Philippines, 4th Quarter 1997, 18–19; 1st Quarter 1998, 13–15.

tion suddenly burst onto the scene in late 1997 as an alarming new development. The liberalization of the previously heavily regulated and subsidized oil industry in February 1997 had been a significant milestone in the broad economic reform drive of the Ramos administration. In the second half of 1997, however, public opposition to the new policy framework began to escalate rapidly when the prices paid by consumers rose dramatically in response to the falling value of the peso coupled with rising prices in world oil markets.

Sensitive to the implications of this for voters with an election drawing near, several members of congress filed suit before the Supreme Court challenging the constitutionality of the deregulation law. The administration and many foreign investors were shocked when the Supreme Court did indeed overturn the law on November 5.[37] The ruling was a major setback for several reasons. First, it threw oil industry pricing and administration into confusion. Second, it raised potentially very serious fiscal problems for the government if, as critics were demanding, some form of subsidization of oil products were reintroduced. Third, as with the income tax legislation, the deregulation of the oil industry was an explicit part of the government's reform obligations to the IMF under the EFF agreement and failure to deliver a bill would jeopardize access to new standby credit facilities. And finally, the episode raised an important question about the ability of the Philippine political system to generate policy reform that was at once timely and credible. Attempting to resolve the situation simply on the basis of executive decree would rectify the oil prices themselves, but would not fix the wider requirement for a credible regulatory solution; a mere decree could be easily reversed. In order to reassure the IMF, oil industry players, and investors more generally, the government needed to relegislate the matter properly, seeking a policy outcome that all veto players would accept and doing so in a fashion that was not subject to challenge on grounds of constitutionality.

From the point of view of an administration nearing the end of its

37. "Oil Investors Freeze Projects after SC Ruling," *Philippine Graphic,* 24 November 1997; "SC Strikes Dead Law on Oil Deregulation," *Philippine Daily Inquirer,* 6 December 1997.

term and desperately struggling to prevent a more extensive investment collapse, this setback could not have come at a worse time. The administration promptly set about redrafting the legislation and renegotiating its passage with the congress in an effort to reaffirm the liberalization of the oil sector before the Christmas break. But the politics of the situation were very difficult: the deregulation of the oil industry had never been a popular move and was even less so now with rapidly rising prices.[38] Furthermore, an upcoming election meant that the whole spectrum of interests—from low-income consumers to firms that would gain or lose from deregulation—was vigorously represented.[39] In the face of such political complexity, the administration was forced to request an extension of the IMF's deadline for the introduction of appropriate legislation. But with regional economic uncertainty reaching new heights, fulfilling the IMF's requirements had become imperative. Again the administration swung into action to encourage both chambers of the congress to move toward a compromise version of the bill that came close enough to the original version of the law and the IMF's core requirements to allow the whole issue to subside.[40] Intense bargaining finally achieved the necessary outcome early in 1998, before congress closed for the electoral campaign. The compromise outcome, together with falling international oil prices in 1998, effectively put the government close enough to where it had been prior to the Supreme Court ruling to enable the whole matter to subside as an issue of market confidence and the management of the economic crisis.[41] Once again, although the process was messy and belated, the net result was satisfactory. The country's political architecture certainly did not facilitate rapid pol-

38. For useful overviews of the substantive issues involved, see Tuano (1998) and "The Oil Deregulation Agenda" (1996).

39. The congressman who had played the lead role in legally challenging the constitutionality of the original deregulation law, Enrique Garcia, championed the cause of a business group that would be hurt by liberalization (Magno 1998, 204–5).

40. "Govt to Seek Extension of IMF Program to Wait for Bill's OK," *Business World* (Manila), 27 January 1998; "Oil Deregulation Bill Needs IMF Okay, Says Singson," *Philippine Daily Inquirer,* 26 January 1998.

41. "House OKs Oil Deregulation Law," *Manila Times,* 13 January 1998; "Senators Start to Yield Ground on New Oil Law," *Manila Times,* 28 January 1997. Economic Intelligence Unit, the Philippines, 1st Quarter 1998, pp. 15–16; 2nd Quarter 1998, pp. 14–17.

icy change, but it was sufficiently flexible to permit change when necessary. It enabled policy makers to salvage what would otherwise have been a very damaging situation at a time of widespread investor nervousness.

The striking point about the Philippine case is the relative coherence and consistency of policy management, even in the face of serious policy setbacks for the administration. Integral to this was the country's political architecture. Unlike Thailand, there were not so many veto players that decisive policy action became all but impossible. Under the institutional configuration in the Philippines, timely policy adjustment was indeed possible if the administration was willing to fight hard. And, viewed from the other side, the constraints on executive action by the bicameral legislature were sufficient to preclude the possibility of radical policy volatility—the syndrome we observe in Malaysia and Indonesia. I am not suggesting that the policy response of the government was in some sense optimal; inevitably there is scope for debate about whether monetary policy settings could have been better targeted and so forth. Nevertheless, in the face of a very severe external economic shock, the Philippine government was able to present a remarkably steady and coherent policy response. Alone among the four cases, the credit rating for the Philippines did not fall sharply throughout the crisis but held steady.[42] Beneath this pattern of governance lay the country's political architecture. Foundational political institutions set the parameters of what was possible in policy terms.

MALAYSIA

Malaysia is the first of our cases that falls at the other extreme of the institutional range, having a political framework that heavily centralizes decision-making power. Recall from the institutional profiles in chapter 3 that, through the lens of veto player analysis, Malaysia had a single collective veto player—Barisan, or, de facto, the UMNO leadership (because it behaved like a single party rather than a coalition of separate parties). With only one veto player, Malaysia's polit-

42. Grenville (1999, 8).

ical framework was conducive to very flexible and decisive policy action. Decisions by the party leadership had a powerful and prompt impact; with no other veto players to constrain the process, its decisions could be translated quickly into law and practice. In this system, policy pronouncements by government leaders—especially the prime minister—were highly consequential. Unlike pronouncements by Chavalit (in Thailand) or even by Ramos (in the Philippines), policy pronouncements by Mahathir were watched very closely because they usually indicated decisive policy action of a sort seldom imaginable for his Philippine and, especially, Thai counterparts. The other consequence of this heavily centralized veto structure was the potential for dangerous policy volatility. Just as there could be strong and decisive policy thrusts in one direction, so too could such action be quickly reversed. Unfortunately, in Malaysia this danger was fully realized as policy responses to the economic situation swung hard one way, then hard the other way, and then hard back again. There was a strong connection between political architecture and the government's overall policy posture in response to the unfolding crisis. With no institutional checks beyond the need to maintain party support, policy could move powerfully and rapidly in almost any direction and at almost any time. This produced profound uncertainty about the future direction of policy. In Thailand, an institutional framework that severely fragmented decision-making power produced policy rigidity. In Malaysia, the problems lay far at the other end of the range—an institutional framework that severely centralized decision-making power, producing the opposite but still deeply problematic pattern of policy volatility.

Malaysia's currency came under serious pressure in July 1997, hot on the heels of the decisions by Bangkok and then Manila to allow their currencies to adjust downward. After a brief and expensive attempt to defend the ringgit by the central bank, Bank Negara Malaysia—involving a sharp upward spike in interest rates and spending an estimated U.S.\$2.9 billion in the currency market[43]—Malaysia accepted that its currency too would have to fall. Once the ringgit had been allowed to fall and the reality of the widening re-

43. Athukorala (1998, 94–95).

gional currency instability became clear, Malaysia faced similar choices about whether to tighten monetary and fiscal policy and whether to tighten prudent arrangements in the financial sector.[44] Malaysia's initial stance on monetary and fiscal policy was clear and in stark contrast to other countries in the region: it was not about to go on a crash course of orthodox macroeconomic austerity. After the decision to let the ringgit fall, interest rates were allowed to return to their earlier levels. There was no concerted effort to use monetary policy to support the currency and guard against inflation (indeed, interest rates in Malaysia were markedly lower than the other countries). Higher interest rates were particularly unwelcome to local firms whose growth had been funded in large measure by local borrowing (in ringgits). Prime Minister, Mahathir, had championed the development of the local corporate sector and was unwilling to see this reversed, not least because many of those who had had access to the most extensive bank lending and were most heavily leveraged were closely allied with the UMNO party leadership and with him in particular.[45]

At the same time, Mahathir began to expound publicly his argument that foreign investors and hedge-fund operators, in particular, were to blame for the roiling Southeast Asian currency markets. Backing up his rhetoric, on July 28 Mahathir declared that the government would take action to prevent speculation against the ringgit and on August 1 the central bank, Bank Negara Malaysia, duly announced limited currency controls on foreigners, with ringgit sales for noncommercial purposes restricted to U.S.$2 million per day. In mid-August, Mahathir defiantly ruled out a more cautious fiscal stance, insisting that the government push ahead with a series of controversial and very large-scale import-dependent infrastructure projects that had become important symbols of developmental pride and involved valuable contracts for firms linked to the party.[46] And

44. A spectrum of useful studies focusing specifically on Malaysia's experiences throughout the crisis are Athukorala (1998), Jomo (1998b, 2001), IMF (1999a, pt. 2, chap. 4), Rasiah (1998), Haggard and Low (1999), and Delhaise (1998, chap. 7).

45. Gomez and Jomo (1997); Searle (1999).

46. "KL Won't Defer Key Mega Projects," *Business Times,* (Singapore), 15 August 1997.

then, in a still more dramatic move, it was announced that off-budget fiscal resources would be deployed in order to intervene in the stock market to hit back at speculators and defend the big Malaysian companies. To this end, on August 27 short-selling of shares in the top one hundred companies was prohibited and a week later it was announced that the Employees Provident Fund (a national pension fund under the central bank) would be tapped to set up a M$60 billion (U.S.$20 billion) fund to purchase shares from domestic investors at a premium above the market rate. As Prema-chandra Athukorala points out, this extraordinary move to discriminate in favor of large (UMNO-connected) firms contributed to a rapid growth in the money supply.[47]

Strong and decisive policy action of this sort, which was unimaginable in Thailand's political system, was quite normal on a priority issue in Malaysia. The prime minister had decided that stiff measures were needed and policy action closely corresponding to his rhetoric followed swiftly. Although the thinking behind these measures may have initially appealed to the UMNO-related firms that were intended to benefit from it, the reaction of the market as a whole was decidedly negative. Mahathir's policy stance was clear but far from reassuring to investors. The ringgit and the stock exchange fell sharply through August. Significant foreign investment was rapidly fleeing. By September 4 the currency had fallen by 15 percent and the stock exchange, having fallen 14 percent in a single week, was at a four-year low. Malaysia's economic situation had suddenly become serious. The political significance of this was quickly apparent and neatly illustrates the collective nature of Malaysia's single-veto-player structure. On September 4, in preparation for a meeting of the UMNO Supreme Council both the finance minister, Anwar Ibrahim, and the UMNO economic godfather, Daim Zainuddin, met with Mahathir and urged adjustments to Mahathir's policy stance.[48] That Anwar—whose ambitions to replace Mahathir simmered just beneath the surface of Malaysian politics—should have divergent

47. Athukorala (1998, 97).
48. "Daim Was the Driver in Mahathir's U-Turn," *Business Times* (Singapore), 16 September 1997; "Thus Spake Mahathir," *Far Eastern Economic Review,* 18 September 1997, 65.

policy preferences was unsurprising. That he should be joined by Daim—a close confidant of Mahathir, the party treasurer, and the foremost figure in the Malaysian corporate world—was much more significant. Mahathir's own supporters in the party were becoming anxious as their personal fortunes declined in tandem with the stock market. In good times, the prime minister's dominance of the cabinet and the party had been far-reaching. But unified advice rooted in party disquiet was a serious issue that no leader could take lightly. In a parliamentary framework of this sort, the political survival of the leader and the control of policy rested on the same thing—support within the party. The party leadership was unhappy with the direction of policy and so change was needed.

At the ensuing party assembly, Mahathir announced what was in effect a policy U-turn, retreating from some unorthodox policy measures. He reversed the ban on short-selling he had launched the day before and also reversed his earlier stance on the big infrastructure projects, conceding now that some of them would have to be delayed in the interests of reassuring nervous investors. These new policies went promptly into effect. Whatever the policy objective, Malaysia's institutional framework allowed government to be agile and decisive, and the government was now promptly delivering the policy adjustments the market was calling for. The content of the new policy was welcome, but was the new policy commitment credible? Having made one U-turn, would the direction of policy now remain stable? With a well-established track record for providing an attractive business environment, investors had come to trust Mahathir's government, but flexible, decisive policy leadership is a two-edged sword. Under pressure, Mahathir had suddenly taken extraordinary anti-foreign-investor measures. Now he was promising to revert back again. Could this repair the damage? Was it believable? As one international investor tersely put it at the time, "The damage has been done. The risk premium of investing in this market will go up."[49] With past behavior no longer a comforting guide to future policy action, investors were left to ponder whether there was anything to prevent the government switching tack again. As a Malaysian business

49. "What Next?" *Far Eastern Economic Review,* 18 September 1997, 62.

leader put it, "What the market wants to see is a consistency in policies so that fund managers can make investment decisions without undue worries."[50]

In a heavily centralized political system there are no guarantees of policy stability. In addition to damaging his government's reputation in the eyes of foreign investors, Mahathir's actions starkly highlighted the potential for policy volatility inherent in Malaysia's political architecture. With only one veto player, decisions could be made quickly and strong policy measures unleashed immediately. But these policy thrusts could be in almost any direction. No matter how good the system's past record, there are inherent policy risks in highly centralized political systems. And as the fabric of the country's political economy was increasingly strained by deteriorating economic circumstances, for both heavyweight UMNO-enmeshed local firms and foreign hedge funds, uncertainty about how the single veto player would behave next became ever greater. Whatever a company's substantive policy preferences, uncertainty was a common concern. Although markets initially rallied in response to the government's policy U-turn, the uptick was short-lived.[51]

Later in the month, the government's policy posture shifted again as the prime minister began to renew his rhetorical attacks on foreign speculators, accusing them of undermining the hard-won development achievements of countries such as Malaysia and calling for the introduction of international controls on capital flows. With market indicators again falling rapidly, ratings agencies began to downgrade Malaysia's foreign and local debt risk, citing the government's failure to tighten monetary policy.[52] In late September, there was a run on the country's largest finance company, MBf Finance, which only subsided when the central bank announced that it would make available funds to cover all depositors. And the budget announced on October 17 received a negative market reception, with critics attacking it for not including any major new commitments to monetary or fiscal discipline while simultaneously handing out cor-

50. "Worst May Be Over for Economy, Mahathir," *Business Times* (Singapore), 10 September 1997, 4.

51. Economist Intelligence Unit, Malaysia, 4th Quarter 1997, 23.

52. Ibid., pp. 23–24.

porate tax cuts, as well as for employing very optimistic growth projections. Its only gesture in the direction of orthodoxy was the announcement of a requirement for banks to increase provisions for bad loans by half a percentage point to 1.5 percent of total lending.[53]

Under the prime minister's direction, policy was determinedly expansionary and sought to restrict short-term foreign investors. But his unorthodox policy approach persistently received a negative market reception and conspicuously failed to stem the slide in business confidence. The economy was heading into very dangerous waters and he was struggling to balance the spectrum of interests that underlay his leadership position. Recognizing the seriousness of the situation, Mahathir reluctantly agreed that other policy options be explored. In policy terms, this implied more swings. And in political terms, this meant ceding more initiative to Finance Minister Anwar Ibrahim who, armed with central bank and IMF advice, was pushing the case for a much more orthodox policy response to the crisis. But this carried risks for Mahathir's position as prime minister because it gave his ambitious deputy the chance to shine and possibly win enough support within the party to challenge for the leadership. In a symbolically dramatic move that served as a hedge against this political risk, Mahathir created a new super-cabinet committee, the National Economic Action Council, bestowing it with unspecified emergency powers. Crucially, he brought in his close ally Daim Zainuddin to play the leading role in the council rather than Finance Minister Anwar. A party heavyweight and the country's most politically connected businessman, Daim was well placed to keep an eye on Anwar. To ensure that his new strategy was fully accepted within the party, Mahathir secured the endorsements of both the UMNO Supreme Council and Barisan as a whole. Only then did he launch it publicly in emergency meetings with business, trade union, and newspaper leaders.[54]

With Anwar at the economic rudder, policy quickly swung hard

53. "No Pain, No Gain," *Financial Times* (London), 20 October 1997; "Tougher, but Not Tough Enough," *Business Times* (Singapore), 20 October 1997; "Mild Medicine," *Far Eastern Economic Review*, 30 October 1997, 61.

54. "Mahathir Holds Briefings on Economy," *Straits Times* (Singapore), 23 November 1997.

around again. In early December, after being approved by the cabinet and with Mahathir's endorsement, Anwar unveiled a major set of strongly orthodox reforms that were widely viewed as the most important policy turning point in a decade.[55] Among the key elements were an 18 percent budget cut, an indefinite postponement of all big infrastructure projects still in the pipeline, a halt to new outbound Malaysian investment (previously a pet project of the prime minister), and an instruction to banks to limit lending only to productive undertakings and not to flinch from cutting support to nonviable firms. This was a stark swing in policy. The stock market surged on the news.

The sharp swing toward economic orthodoxy was infused with intense political implications; it suggested that Anwar, who in the preceding months had been limited to cleaning up after Mahathir's outbursts on restraining global capital, had now succeeded in prying significant policy initiative away from the prime minister. Through December and the early part of 1998, Anwar pushed ahead with the orthodox agenda. To strengthen the financial sector, Anwar pushed for mergers among banks and finance companies and announced tighter prudential measures for the banks and brokerage firms.[56] Particularly important were the deliberate moves to tighten monetary policy, with the central bank pushing interest rates up through the first and second quarters of the year.[57] One market analyst described Anwar's reforms as "a sea change in the way Malaysia addresses its economic problems . . . essentially IMF reform without the IMF," but warned that "confidence will not return if people still suspect that the prime minister might reverse the decisions in a few weeks or months down the line."[58] The underlying questions about

55. "Bold Steps to Get Economy on Track," *Business Times* (Singapore), 6 December 1997; "New Measures Necessary: Dr M," *Business Times* (Malaysia), 8 December 1997; "Hit the Brakes," *Far Eastern Economic Review,* 18 December 1997, 14–15.

56. "Anwar: Merge to Boost Resilience," *Business Times,* (Malaysia), 9 December 1997; "Pull Together: Malaysia Orders Finance Companies to Merge," *Far Eastern Economic Review,* 15 January 1998, 52.

57. "Central Bank Hands Out Carrots and Sticks," *Straits Times* (Singapore), 26 March 1998.

58. "Malaysia Not Asking for a Bailout," *Nikkei Weekly,* 15 December 1997, 22.

policy stability and credibility had not gone away; they were embedded in the country's political architecture.

While Anwar's deflationary macroeconomic policies and tougher prudential arrangements in the financial sector were winning praise from the IMF, Mahathir, in conjunction with Daim, was working to ensure that the tighter financial environment did not bring down the corporate empires of key party supporters. Bailouts and assistance measures of various sorts were provided to a number of major firms; most notably, the state oil company came to the aid of the prime minister's oldest son's business group.[59] The underlying tension between the two opposing policy strategies came to a head as 1998 progressed.

Anwar's position was weakened by the fact that official data and ratings agency assessments revealed that, far from improving, Malaysia's economic conditions were deteriorating further. Despite his austerity measures and declarations about sound economic policy paving the way for recovery, the economy continued to slow, even contracting in the first quarter of 1998. And with this, nonperforming loans began to rise rapidly.[60] Anwar continued to call for patience, urging perseverance with tight monetary and fiscal settings and strict bank foreclosure on bad debtors. But because this approach failed to yield evident fruit and generated howls of pain from cash-starved firms (not least the powerful firms linked to the party hierarchy), Anwar was becoming politically vulnerable. Frustrated by the lack of economic results and sensing a political opportunity, through the second quarter of the year Mahathir and Daim began publicly to contradict Anwar's policy signals. With growing force, they called his orthodox efforts into doubt, openly suggesting that it might be better to ease interest rates and revive public spending to support the previously shelved big infrastructure projects.[61]

What were investors to think? Where was policy heading this time? The volatility of the policy environment was becoming less and less tolerable for investors. As one businessman succinctly stated the problem, "There's a lot of risk that's not quantifiable because of the

59. Jomo (1998a, 186–89); Haggard and Low (1999, 10–17).
60. Economist Intelligence Unit, Malaysia, 3rd Quarter 1998, pp. 18, 23.
61. "Read the Signs," *Far Eastern Economic Review,* 18 June 1998, 18–21.

flip-flops."[62] This became a constant refrain in the face of the strong
but highly changeable policy responses coming from the government: in July and August 1997, policy signals had pointed strongly in
an unorthodox and expansionary direction; in September they reversed direction briefly before again moving back in an expansionary direction; from December through February they swung around
again to point strongly in an orthodox contractionary direction; and
now, in the second quarter of 1998, they were pointing strongly in
both directions at once as the two leading ministers in the party
tugged at different policy levers.

This new pattern of strongly conflicting signals was anomalous, arising from what had by now evolved into a deep and unresolved political division inside the single collective veto player. In simple terms, it
was unclear who was going to control the party. Did Mahathir or Anwar now enjoy the support of the majority of party members? The ambiguity in policy reflected the ambiguity in the balance of power inside
the party. At this point, it appeared possible that either might come
out on top—Mahathir was not yet certain he could squash his ambitious deputy, and Anwar was not yet certain he could topple his party
leader. During the hiatus they both pursued their diverging policy
goals. And because there were no other veto players to check unilateral action, they could both do so vigorously. In effect, the single veto
player was speaking strongly with two voices. Or, in more concrete
terms, because control of policy was so heavily centralized, whatever
the cabinet wanted was enacted expeditiously; but with the cabinet—
indeed the party as a whole—not yet willing or able to choose between
the two men, the policies of both were vigorously implemented
through the different executive agencies they each controlled.

Quite apart from its negative impact on the economy, politically
this standoff could not last. A looming party assembly in June was the
natural venue for a showdown. An already tense situation was pushed
up to fever pitch by the stunning economic meltdown in neighbor-
ing Indonesia and then the dramatic fall of Suharto in late May. This
strongly colored the discourse in Malaysia. Anwar supporters seized
this window of political opportunity to begin drawing parallels be-

62. "Mixed Signals: Dynamic Duo Relays Conflicting Economic Measures," *Far
Eastern Economic Review,* 21 May 1998, 24.

tween Mahathir and Suharto. At the UMNO general assembly in mid-June they openly called for an end to nepotism and corruption. But despite the difficulties, Mahathir was in a stronger position within the party than Anwar. In the face of this all but openly declared challenge to his authority, Mahathir now acted swiftly to exploit the full institutional powers of the prime ministership and the party presidency to move against his opponents.[63] In a party purge rolling through July and August, Mahathir forced the resignation of Anwar supporters from key posts, brought Daim formally into the cabinet and vested him with special economic powers, and squeezed out the governor and deputy governor of central bank.[64] With the key Anwar supporters eliminated, many others scurried for cover.

As Anwar was pushed to the margins and unity of purpose restored inside the party, the ambiguity in economic policy quickly disappeared. And so the direction of economic policy swung hard around yet again.[65] Monetary policy was relaxed, allowing interest rates to fall. Recently tightened bank statutory reserve requirements were again loosened. The government also signaled that public spending would now be pumped up again and that measures would be introduced to assist firms in distress. And, in his most dramatic move, as international ratings agencies continued to downgrade Malaysia, at the end of August Mahathir ordered the halt of all international trading in Malaysian stocks, the suspension of currency convertibility, and the lifting and pegging of the exchange rate. A day after decoupling the economy from the international financial system, Mahathir fired Anwar and had him arrested soon after. Malaysia's sovereign rating fell to junk status, but this no longer mattered because the economy was insulated from the international financial markets.[66]

63. "Tactical Victory," *Far Eastern Economic Review,* 2 July 1998.

64. "Mahathir Consolidates Position as Party Chief," *Business Times* (Singapore), 22 June 1998; "Mahathir Outflanks Anwar in Power Play," *Nikkei Weekly,* 6 July 1998; "Heir Unapparent," *Far Eastern Economic Review,* 27 August 1998, 16–17.

65. "Dr M Confirms Change of Economic Course on the Cards," *Business Times* (Singapore), 26 June 1998.

66. "Mahathir Ignores the Requirements of the International Investment Community," *Financial Times,* 6 July 1998; "Bank Negara Eases Monetary Policy," *Business Times* (Malaysia), 1 August 1998; "Mahathir Introduces Strict Currency Controls," *Financial Times,* 2 September 1998.

The overall pattern of policy management exhibited by Malaysia as it sought to respond to the unfolding regional economic crisis stands in stark contrast to that of both Thailand and the Philippines. Once we look beyond Mahathir's rhetoric, the most striking feature of this pattern of behavior was the wild swings from one side of the policy dial to the other. And then back again. And again. There is a strong connection between this pattern of policy volatility and the configuration of the country's political architecture. Such strong surges in one policy direction and then the other and then back again would not have been possible in Thailand or the Philippines. The existence of other veto players prevented this volatility in Thailand and substantially constrained it in the Philippines, so that policy actions would have been neither so strong nor so varied. This was not simply a problem of the appropriate policy mix; that philosophical question remains the subject of serious debate among Malaysian and international economists. More fundamentally, this was a problem of uncertainty arising from policy volatility. A complaint at the time captured the fundamental problem investors faced: "The political situation is highly unsatisfactory. We've seen constant U-turns and doubling back on policy in recent months. If the capital controls don't work, will he reverse himself again?"[67] Investors of all sorts had come to trust the Malaysian government because of its track record of providing an attractive business environment. In a sense, Malaysia's reputation, built on past actions, served as a veil shrouding the great potential for policy volatility embedded in the country's political framework. But when the storm of currency instability came to Malaysia from Thailand and the Philippines and the country's political system was placed under severe strain, the deep vulnerabilities in Malaysian governance were unveiled and plain for all to see. Confronted by the naked problem of policy volatility, investors found Malaysia's reputation alone scant comfort. Rapid and radical policy reversals—made possible by the political institutional framework—turned what should have been a difficult but manageable economic adjustment into a disaster.

67. "After the Fall," *Far Eastern Economic Review,* 17 September 1998, 11.

INDONESIA

The Indonesian case is an even more extreme version of the Malaysian story of the severe centralization of decision-making power leading to a deeply problematic pattern of policy volatility. Like its Malaysian counterpart, the Indonesian government had enjoyed a reputation for generally sound macroeconomic management; despite widespread corruption, in the face of major economic destabilization it had repeatedly demonstrated itself to be capable of undertaking far-reaching structural reforms rapidly. Indonesia's political architecture provided for an even more extreme concentration of decision-making power than in Malaysia. Viewed through the analytical lens of the veto player framework, Indonesia like Malaysia, had only one veto player. But recall from chapter 3 that, in contrast to Malaysia where this was a collective entity (the ruling party), in Indonesia it was a single person, the president. To be sure, Mahathir was a very dominant figure in Malaysian politics, but Suharto, unlike Mahathir, did not need to pay attention to his position in a political party. In addition, of course, the more authoritarian nature of politics in Indonesia further heightened the president's personal dominance of the political system. Indonesia thus presents an even more striking contrast with the political framework of the Philippines, to say nothing of the very fragmented framework in Thailand. And the consequences of this extreme institutional configuration for the overall pattern of governance shows very clearly in the way that Indonesia responded to the crisis. Indonesia's political architecture enabled policy makers to respond in a very flexible and decisive manner, permitting a swift resolution of a problem, but it also carried with it a powerful concomitant potential for unchecked policy volatility.

Once the Thai baht had depreciated, as with other regional currencies, it was inevitable that the Indonesian rupiah would have to adjust.[68] The government responded swiftly to this situation.

68. For more detailed discussions on the wider economics and politics of the crisis in Indonesia, see McLeod (1998a), Robison and Rosser (1998), Soesastro and Basri (1998), Pincus and Ramli (1998), Hill (1999), Hamilton-Hart (2000), Simandjuntak (1999), IMF (1999a, pt. 2, chap. 2), and World Bank (1998c).

Whereas Malaysia initially pursued a determinedly nonorthodox policy approach, Indonesia did the reverse. In a preemptive move, on
July 11 the central bank, Bank Indonesia, widened the daily trading
band of the rupiah from 8 percent to 12 percent, and then, once it
became clear that this would be inadequate to contain the pressure
created by firms with unhedged foreign borrowings rushing to buy
dollars, on August 14 it announced the rupiah would be cut completely loose and allowed to float freely. From this point, the government's policy response quickly moved into high gear. The president
set the tone with a sober assessment of the financial instability in his
August 17 independence day speech. Across the policy spectrum,
strong response measures were unveiled in a bid to shore up confidence in the government's preparedness to tackle the situation head
on. The first and most important moves came with monetary and fiscal policy. In mid-August the government introduced a very sharp liquidity squeeze in an effort to encourage investors to hold rupiah
deposits. Following a strategy Jakarta had employed successfully in
earlier years to deal with currency instability, the central bank moved
to push up interest rates, and separately the finance minister ordered
state enterprises to transfer deposits from commercial banks to the
central bank. Going even further, the finance minister actually froze
all government spending for two weeks.[69] Combined, these measures
dramatically drained liquidity from the interbank market, sending
interest rates extremely high. The aim was to demonstrate the seriousness of governmental purpose to the markets. By showing that it
was quite prepared to introduce bracing adjustment measures, the
government sought to minimize panicked trading in the rupiah. If
investors could be encouraged to hold rupiahs again, the currency's
fall could be checked and wider economic dislocation avoided.

To add credibility to these efforts on the monetary policy front, the
government sought to show that it would accept painful cutbacks on
the fiscal front. To this end, it announced expenditure cuts and new
taxes on luxury goods to ensure a stable budgetary position. Significantly, the government also signaled that a number of very costly and

69. I learned of the quiet, if drastic, move to temporarily freeze all government
payments from Soedradjad Djiwandono, governor of the central bank during the crisis (interview by author, San Diego, Calif., 14 January 1999).

controversial infrastructure projects would be postponed and that a second cluster would be reviewed. The deferral of the big infrastructure projects was important symbolically because this provided further assurance of the government's determination to pursue an orthodox fiscal strategy and suggested a willingness to cut back on the excesses of the president's children and of Suharto cronies who were involved in many of these projects. In the financial sector, the government announced the lifting of restrictions on foreign ownership of shares for companies listed on the Jakarta stock exchange and the central bank signaled that it would look at closing a number of struggling banks. Other flagged measures included a tariff cut on a range of industrial inputs with a view to assisting exporters.[70]

These were tried and tested moves straight out of the government's policy playbook from past economic crises. And, indeed, the rupiah stabilized in September. Market commentators applauded the government's decisive manner and orthodox orientation.[71] As the *Far Eastern Economic Review* put it in September, "Anyone following Southeast Asia's currency crisis could not have helped noticing the stark contrast in official reactions among Malaysia, Thailand, and Indonesia. Where Kuala Lumpur lashed out at speculators and Bangkok struggled unconvincingly to deal with the new financial order, Jakarta kept its head, acting like the mature manager investors look for."[72] This was a familiar and reassuring pattern for investors. Although Suharto's regime was notorious for pervasive corruption and indulgent policy practices when economic conditions were good, it had a reputation for being willing and able to do whatever was necessary to repair the situation during times of economic crisis. Through the first three months of the crisis (July–September) this was exactly what seemed to be happening. The government unleashed very strong policy responses. Indeed, some argue it pushed

70. "Indonesia Lists Major Projects to be Postponed," *Business Times* (Singapore), 24 September 1997; "Really Cool," *Far Eastern Economic Review*, 18 September 1997.
71. "Action Faction: Indonesia's Economic-Crisis Team Pushes Reform," *Far Eastern Economic Review*, 4 September 1997; "In Battle for Investors, This Is No Contest: Amid a Crisis, Indonesia Opens Up and Thrives as Malaysia Stumbles," *Asian Wall Street Journal*, 5 September 1997.
72. "Really Cool," 66–67.

too strongly in a contractionary direction in its monetary policy in July and August (even before the IMF was called in), greatly compounding problems in the financial and corporate sectors.[73]

But even more damaging than this initial, very powerfully contractionary policy surge were the conflicting signals or swings in policy that were to follow. An early example of this was exchange rate policy. After abandoning its attempt to let the rupiah float within a set price band in July, the government announced the rupiah was cut completely free. Before long, however, the central bank began to intervene actively in foreign exchange markets, buying up rupiahs whenever the currency came under serious selling pressure. The government had, in effect, simply reversed course. Was the currency to be allowed to adjust to market pressures freely or was the government going to try to manage the exchange rate indirectly? What was to stop the government changing its mind on other policy measures? As time went on, this question was asked increasingly.

With continuing pressure on the rupiah, the government called for IMF assistance in early October. By the end of the month, it had signed a sweeping agreement for up to $23 billion worth of financial support. Under the terms of the agreement, Indonesia committed itself to an intensification of the strategy it had already begun. Jakarta moved much faster than Bangkok or Manila in collaborating with the IMF. Almost immediately it began implementing measures for the closure of sixteen banks, the abolition of several big import monopolies, the reduction of tariffs on industrial import tariffs, a cost-cutting review of big-spending state-owned strategic industries, and the removal of entry barriers for foreigners to wholesale and distribution activities. Many of these measures promised to hack at the business privileges of Suharto's relatives and key cronies.[74] Again, this was reminiscent of past episodes of severe external economic shock, when,

73. Ross McLeod (1998b; Fane and McLeod 1999), an Australian economist, later developed this into a cogent critique; for some early expressions of concern along these lines, see Rizal Ramli's criticisms in the press, in "Indonesia on a Liquidity Tight-Rope," *Business Times* (Singapore), 12 September 1997.

74. "Indonesia and IMF Agree on Reform Package," *Jakarta Post*, 1 November 1997; "Government Shuts 16 Banks in First Reform Move," *Jakarta Post*, 2 November 1997; "Indonesia Reaches Out to IMF to Combat Loss of Confidence," *Asian Wall Street Journal*, 7–8 November 1997.

as in the mid-1980s, Suharto had authorized sweeping reforms, including temporary but significant cutbacks to the business interests of relatives and cronies.[75]

Compared to what was happening in the Philippines and Thailand, the speed and scope of Jakarta's adjustment measures were stunning. Commenting on the stark differences for the IMF in engaging the Thai and Indonesian political systems, one investment analyst remarked, "In Thailand there are so many interests to serve. With the Indonesians, I think the IMF thought they could get things done."[76] The massive centralization of authority made it possible for Indonesia to do this; everything could be handled executively, and once Suharto gave his assent there were no institutional actors capable of reviewing, much less vetoing, policy action.

But as we saw in the Malaysian case, the heavy centralization of veto authority makes possible strong action in one direction and also its rapid reversal. As November progressed and the economic pressure mounted, this quickly emerged as a fundamental problem. No sooner had the government begun unleashing these orthodox policy measures than it also began taking powerful actions pulling in precisely the opposite direction. As in Malaysia, an early instance of this was a reversal of the decision to shelve big-ticket infrastructure projects. In the flurry of activity implementing the terms of the IMF agreement, Suharto also signed a decree giving the go-ahead anew to eight of the big infrastructure projects that had been postponed in September, as well as to seven of the projects that were being held for review.[77]

Where was government policy headed? This was a disturbing reversal. And it brought into clearer focus the danger embedded in the country's political framework: Suharto was the sole veto player; if he chose to change his mind, there was nothing anyone could do to stop him. More followed. Within a short period of the closure of his bank,

75. MacIntyre (1992).

76. Quoted in "Big Is Best: Indonesia's Rescue Draws on the Thai Experience," *Far Eastern Economic Review,* 13 November 1997, 68–69.

77. "Suharto Gives Go-Ahead to Some Projects," *Asian Wall Street Journal,* 7–8 November 1997; "Fifteen Projects Allowed to Continue after Review," *Jakarta Post,* 8 November 1997.

Suharto's second son stood before the news cameras gloating that he had taken over another bank and was back in business. The next day, November 21, the head of the Chamber of Commerce told the media that Suharto had agreed that some $5 billion provided by the Singapore government for currency stabilization could now be used to bail out struggling Indonesian companies. Not only did this go against the intentions of the Singapore government, it breached the spirit of the IMF agreement, which was pointedly against corporate and bank bailouts. The government subsequently issued a denial, but the damage had been done.[78]

Policy became increasingly volatile. As these various developments unfolded in the media through November, uncertainty about the policy environment mounted and the slide of the rupiah accelerated. But perhaps the most devastating reversal of all was what amounted to a 180-degree swing in monetary policy starting in November as a result of a desperate bailout of the banking sector. The banks were by now in dreadful shape, having been battered by an extremely tight liquidity squeeze, rising nonrepayment of loans, and, since the closure of the sixteen banks, panicked depositor withdrawals. As the banking sector slid toward insolvency, the president declared there would be no more bank closures and the central bank was forced to make special liquidity credit facilities available to keep distressed banks afloat. Even more than the bailouts of the well-connected Thai finance companies, this move proved to have disastrous macroeconomic consequences. Whatever the government's intentions, the result of this move was that banks rapidly lined up for assistance, with crony banks returning repeatedly and drawing vast sums. The largest such bank, Bank Central Asia (BCA), alone soaked up Rp35 trillion (roughly U.S.$7 billion in late 1997 prices), amassing liquidity support equivalent to more than 500 percent of its capital.[79] As was later

78. "Jakarta's Mixed Signals Erode Confidence," *Asian Wall Street Journal,* 11 December 1997.

79. "Govt to Blame for State of Banking Industry," *Jakarta Post,* 25 August 1998; "Govt to Recapitalize BCA, Three Other Banks," *Jakarta Post,* 1 October 1998. It is unclear exactly how much money was released through this liquidity credit operation. According to the official figures, the total may have reached Rp92 trillion, in which case BCA consumed more than one-third of this on its own (McLeod 1998a,

publicly confirmed, crony banks immediately misappropriated the liquidity credits, siphoning them out of the country and speculating against the rupiah. This massive expansion in the money supply from November on had devastating consequences. Notwithstanding the continued high bank-lending rates, it led to a rapid upward revision of inflationary expectations, encouraging capital flight.

Policy signals had become hopelessly changeable. The government was taking very strong policy steps, but they frequently represented a negation or outright reversal of earlier moves. This was an impossible position for investors; the wild policy swings were completely destroying the investment environment for crony and non-crony firms alike.[80]

Indonesia's situation began to deteriorate alarmingly through November and December. By the end of 1997, the currency had lost 54 percent of its precrisis value, already exceeding the low points of all other crisis-affected economies. From this point on, the situation spiraled quickly out of control. The budget announced on January 6—widely viewed as the last chance to retrieve matters—received a very negative local and international reception, being seen as unrealistic and as further backsliding by the government on earlier commitments to the IMF.[81] Outright panic set in as hoarding of food staples began, with individual consumers as well as big companies dumping the currency. As the currency went into free fall, investor confidence was utterly routed. There was, quite simply, no basis for confidence in the government; there was no way of knowing where policy would swing next. As one local businessman put it at the time, "If people trusted the government they wouldn't be panicking like this."[82]

With world leaders telephoning Suharto, top U.S. Treasury and IMF officials rushed to Jakarta. Treasury Deputy Secretary Lawrence

n. 6 p. 48). See also the public report of the Center for Banking Crisis, *Buku Putuh* (Jilid 1), Jakarta, 1999.

80. I have explored the equivalent difficulties the government created for firms regardless of their connections in Haggard and MacIntyre (2001).

81. "Indonesia's Worrying Budget," *Asian Wall Street Journal*, 9–10 January 1998; "IMF Set to Review Indonesia's Budget Proposals," *Financial Times*, 8 January 1998.

82. Quoted in "Indonesia: Ground Zero," *Far Eastern Economic Review*, 22 January 1998, 14–17.

Summers bluntly summarized international advice: "It will be crucial for Indonesia to carry through on policy commitments it has made in the context of the IMF program."[83] Such advice was all very well, but how could any government credibly commit when there were no institutional checks on unilateral presidential power? There was no basis for the government to tie its own hands.

Within a matter of days, a revised agreement with the IMF had been drawn up that provided for a truly stunning list of economic reforms. This was a last-ditch effort to prop up the regime's standing with investors by seeking to demonstrate renewed commitment to making cuts where it hurt the most. Although Suharto promptly signed the new agreement on January 15, it was all too late. By this stage the government's credibility with investors inside and outside Indonesia was irreparably damaged. The promise to implement a reform package of unprecedented scope failed to impress; nobody believed it would be done.[84] Suharto's commitments were no longer of any value.

The latent policy volatility that had long been embedded in the country's radically centralized political architecture was now fully exposed. Factors that had in previous years mitigated investors' concerns about the risk of policy volatility—strong rates of return, the government's reputation for reliable macroeconomic management, and the disciplining effect of an open capital account—had all been swept away by these catastrophic circumstances.[85] Investors were left with the stark reality that there could be no solid foundation for confidence in a political framework with no institutional checks on executive power—the president could reverse commitments almost as fast as he made them.

83. Quoted in "U.S. Warning to Indonesia," *New York Times*, 8 January 1998, Business section.

84. "Sweeping Reforms Unveiled by Jakarta and IMF Fail to Impress Markets," *Asian Wall Street Journal*, 16–17 January 1998.

85. Elsewhere, I have argued that we can see these factors underpinning Indonesia's prior ability to attract high levels of private investment despite the fundamental governance problem embedded in its political architecture. But these proved to be weak reeds in the face of a storm of this magnitude (see MacIntyre 2001b).

As in Malaysia, the very heavy concentration of decision-making power meant that policy could be adjusted very quickly. In Indonesia, the government responded to the onset of currency instability by very rapidly pursuing a strict, orthodox policy path—even before the IMF arrived. Monetary and fiscal settings swung hard in a contractionary direction. But there was no institutional monitoring or coordinating—much less a veto—of any of the actions the executive took. And as the consequences of early powerful policy action began to work through the economy—reinforced, as elsewhere, by ongoing external buffeting—the problem became multidimensional. As were the other governments, Jakarta was fighting fires on many fronts, struggling to cope with urgent and competing demands from diverse constituencies. But whereas Ramos and Chavalit had to obtain agreement from other veto players for action to proceed on many issues—and even Mahathir had to have regard for his party colleagues—Suharto could unilaterally order strong and immediate action on any front. And so, by the fourth quarter of 1997 the overall policy picture had become increasingly conflicted and erratic. This was not a simple story of policy error or even venality (although both were certainly present); more fundamentally, it was an unconstrained presidency taking powerful but conflicting steps in response to the increasingly powerful and conflicting problems of diverse constituencies. The net effect was severe policy volatility. The institutional framework did not cause this syndrome on its own—we need to factor in other elements for the complete story—but it could not have happened without it.

Promises made one day were reversed the next. Projects were suspended and then reinstated. The currency was floated freely and then the central bank intervened heavily in the currency markets. Banks were closed and then reopened under a new name. Monetary policy was severely contractionary and then it was radically expansionary. With policy signals fluctuating so wildly and with there being no institutional mechanism for the government to make credible policy commitments, it is scarcely surprising that there was rapid and total collapse in investment. Investors had no basis for predicting government policy and no basis for trusting government promises. Exit was the only reasonable option. The same radically centralized institutional framework that enabled this volatile pattern of governance also allowed Suharto to cling to power for several more months. But the economic dislocation set in motion by the earlier destruction of investor confidence eventually triggered mass protests, the fragmentation of the elite and, finally, Suharto's fall in late May 1998. In the wake of all the trauma and devastation, redesigning the country's political architecture was every bit as urgent as economic reconstruction.

THE CASES COMPARED

In this chapter I have empirically traced the policy behavior in four comparable cases in response to the 1997–98 Asian economic crisis, highlighting distinctive governance syndromes. The overall pattern of policy management in three of the cases—Thailand, on one hand, and Malaysia and Indonesia, on the other—corresponded strongly to the generalized patterns of problematic governance, policy rigidity and policy volatility. Analytically, in each case I have connected these particular patterns of policy management with the national political architectures, arguing that we can reasonably view the institutional configuration of decision making in each case as essential for understanding what happened. In terms of theory development, I have suggested that these cases can be viewed as useful illustrations of my general argument about the implications of national political architecture for governance. This simple model—the power concentration paradox—turns out to be a remarkably good predictor of how these different political systems performed under stress. Extreme institutional configurations did indeed correlate with the particular problematic patterns of policy management identified in the power concentration paradox model. The Philippines, located in from the two extremes, did not exhibit either of the seriously problematic patterns of governance.

In highlighting the causal connection between institutions and governance, there is much that I have simplified and even omitted. Parsimony comes at a price. There are, of course, other factors affecting the story of why the overall patterns of policy were the way they were in these four cases. More detailed accounts could be constructed that would pick up on the nature and effects of particular political alliances, patterns of business-government relations, the ideological disposition of particular people, and the precise economic circumstances of particular industries and sectors. I take this as given. My claim is that the level of parsimony here is both reasonable and helpful. It is reasonable because of the underlying comparability of the cases (see chap. 1)—on the issues that matter here the cases are remarkably comparable; the differences lie in variables that are of a lesser order. And it is helpful because it allows us to illuminate the powerful residual causal effect exerted by basic institutions, an effect that might otherwise be obscured by the complex and shifting reality that we summarize with the word "politics."

Having said this, we also need to squarely address some of the limitations of institutionally focused analysis. I have identified patterns of policy management and argued that they are powerfully connected to institutional configurations. But institutions, by themselves, do not cause these policy outcomes. Indeed, institutions by themselves cause very little at all. It is the interests and the ideas that lie behind them that animate politics. Consider Malaysia and Indonesia. Certainly the governments of these countries had track records of strong and decisive policy management, but they did not routinely flip-flop on policy week after week, year after year. The national political architecture made serious policy volatility very much more likely than in the Philippines and Thailand, but it did not compel it. Whether a leader sitting atop a framework that severely concentrates decision-making power does in fact behave in a volatile fashion at any given moment depends on a complex totality of factors shaping individual decisions that, in an important sense, may not ultimately be knowable. What we do know is that the potential for such an outcome was embedded in the political architectures of these countries, and that, as economic and then political pressures mounted, the full potential for policy volatility was laid bare for all to see, with very costly consequences.

We can illustrate this point equally well with either of the other two cases. Consider Thailand. Although other governments operating under that political architecture certainly earned reputations for policy gridlock and snail's pace reform,[86] this was not an inevitable outcome. Indeed, we can identify some examples of policy change proceeding reasonably smoothly (e.g., financial deregulation in the early 1990s). But such cases are very few and far between and are dependent on rare situations of high preference alignment among all the coalition partners. In the absence of this, the potential for policy rigidity embedded in Thailand's political architecture was all too easily exposed. Or consider the interesting intermediate case of the Philippines. Although its having a political framework that was located in from the extremes made the gross governance syndromes much less likely, this by no means guaranteed a happy outcome.

Here it is useful to compare the Philippines with South Korea, another Asian country located toward the center of the range. As my model predicts, South Korea did not exhibit either of the two deeply problematic policy syndromes, nevertheless, during the critical months of 1997 it did fall victim to a set of circumstantial political problems. Kim Young Sam found himself in an extreme lame-duck status, with the usual effect of an approaching election compounded by severe damage to his reputation due to debilitating personal scandal and deep splits between him and his party.[87] But when the new administration of Kim Dae Jung came to power, these circumstantial problems were out of the way and his administration was able to make substantial headway in bringing about important policy adjustment.[88]

For our purposes, institutions are best understood as crucial enabling conditions rather than as determinants. The importance of institutions is their intervening effect, with the rules of political engagement constraining the outcomes of contests between conflicting sets of interests and ideas. By structuring the terms of engagement,

---

86. Recall that this did not apply to the caretaker administrations of Anand or the earlier Prem administrations, during which there were important differences in the institutional framework.

87. Haggard (2000, 55–59, 100–107); Haggard and MacIntyre (2001).

88. Kim's ability to affect change continued beyond this special period between the election and his inauguration, and into 1998 as well.

national political architecture exerts a powerful systemic influence on the outcomes of political contests. And crisis episodes are particularly opportune vehicles for studying these effects because it is in times of extreme political pressure—when everyone, from banker to laborer, is seeking to haul on all available political levers in an effort to secure urgent policy gratification—that the capabilities and consequences of national political architectures are likely to be most fully exposed.

The credible commitments literature alerts us to the problems of Malaysia-like or Indonesia-like situations; the decisiveness literature alerts us to the problems of Thailand-like situations. But there has been no coherent theory that explains why these different institutional settings can become so problematic for governance, or why a Philippines-like situation is much less so. My argument does. Exposing the contrasting institutional foundations of these governance syndromes and recognizing the U-shaped relationship that lies at the heart of the power concentration paradox provides the missing theoretical link that enables us to connect basic variation in political institutions with elemental aspects of governance in a systematic way.

CHAPTER 5

Political Architecture and Change

In chapter 4 I used Southeast Asian policy reform (responses to the 1997–98 financial crisis) to illustrate and support my argument about the implications of national political architecture for governance. In this chapter I go a step further, tracing Southeast Asian struggles over political reform in the wake of the economic panic and linking these back to my argument about the effects of institutional configuration.

It did not initially occur to me that processes of institutional change might speak strongly to a study of the effects of institutions. After all, analytically, it is the institutional framework that I have been holding constant to highlight its effects. But institutions—even the most foundational political rules—are not set in stone, immutable for all time. Constitutional changes as well as organic realignments of the party system happen from time to time. In varying degrees, all four of our Southeast Asian cases have seen an intense struggle for political reform, partly as a result of the financial crisis. Indonesia and Thailand carried out far-reaching processes of institutional redesign. In both the Philippines and Malaysia the pressures for political change were defeated, albeit in starkly differing circumstances. The further I investigated this, the more forcefully I was struck by the way in which the processes of institutional change unfolded and especially by the direction and overall pattern of institutional change and nonchange. The cases that underwent the greatest change were those located at the extremes of the range of distribution of decision-making power. Moreover, the thrust of their reforms was to pull them in from the extreme positions that they had occupied. The Philippines, which was already located away from the extremes and toward the center of the range, consciously resisted what were seen as dangerous plans for institutional reform. These outcomes, I suddenly realized, offer an unexpected confirmation of my core argument. Although Malaysia presents a partial exception to the pattern, the wider pattern seems to be more than a coincidence.

My purpose in this chapter is twofold. First, I empirically construct coherent and systematic analytical narratives of the dramatic struggles over political change in our four Southeast Asian cases. This is no small undertaking; indeed this is the first attempt at a comparative account of these issues across Southeast Asia. In this, as in the previous chapter, I consciously opt for constructing a lean set of stories; I provide only as much detail as is strictly necessary to make my case and forgo the opportunity to illuminate the many interesting tangents that branch from the central topic. Second, I tie the analysis of the dynamics of institutional reform in these four countries back to the relationship between political architecture and governance. The first task is time-consuming and is of greatest interest to readers who follow Southeast Asia for its own sake. Readers interested primarily in the theoretical relationship may choose to skip to the final section of the chapter to see how I tie the overall patterns of change (and nonchange) in the political architecture of these four countries back to my core claims about the extent of the dispersal of decision-making power and governance. The payoff for me after the long journey to construct these narratives of institutional reform was, suddenly, to become aware of patterns that had previously escaped me despite a long-standing interest in the region. It was only through comparison that the patterns emerged.

INSTITUTIONAL REFORM

Institutional reform is difficult. New political frameworks do not fall from the heavens and slide directly into place. They are the product of debate and struggle—often violent struggle. They are ideas

about how politics should be organized that are articulated, promoted, entrenched, and then defended by a coalition of actors seeking to advance certain interests. The reason people fight about
political institutions is precisely that they privilege some values and
interests over others. Institutions can thus very much be thought of
as "congealed preferences," as William Riker engagingly put it.[1]
Once congealed, they are not easily remolded.

The fact that institutions are usually difficult to alter is part of what
makes them important. Indeed, this is almost axiomatic because if institutions were easily changeable they would not be worth fighting
over in practical terms and would be unremarkable as causal variables in theoretical terms. Douglass North has written of a nested hierarchy of institutions running from constitutions to statutes and
common laws all the way to individual contracts and notes that, of all
formal institutions, foundational political rules are usually the most
difficult to alter.[2] And yet, from time to time, political architecture
does undergo change.

In broad terms, there are two sets of problems that must be overcome if the basic political rules of a state are to be reformed: difficulties of dislodging the existing institutional framework and
difficulties of establishing a new framework. Difficulties of dislodging can arise because the defenders of the existing institutional
framework resist fiercely or because the existing framework was designed in a way that makes it stubbornly tamper-proof long after its
defenders have declined or disappeared. Difficulties in establishing
a new institutional framework can arise because of a protracted struggle to achieve a new dominant consensus or because of flaws in the
design of the new framework that prove so dysfunctional that it
quickly collapses.

How might the existing political architecture be dislodged? Kathy
Thelen has observed that "Institutions rest on a set of ideational and
material foundations that, if shaken, open possibilities for change."[3]
In this, she is pointing to the most common explanation among political scientists for major institutional change: a critical historical

1. Riker (1980, 445).
2. North (1990, 47).
3. Thelen (1999, 397).

juncture at which a crisis or dramatic shock—such as a war or a radical economic downturn—knocks the system out of equilibrium, rupturing the economic and political alliances that underlie the existing institutional order and opening the door for new actors seeking to alter the rules of the game. Or as John Ikenberry put it, "The importance of crisis stems from the intransigence of political institutions. . . . Extraordinary events prompt not just policy change, but also changes in institutional structure."[4]

Dislodging the old institutional order is one hurdle, forging some measure of agreement about the establishment of the new framework is the next. Redesigning the basic rules of national politics can be an especially difficult category of institutional reform. This is not simply because the stakes are so high, but more subtly because politicians are frequently both the subjects and the objects of change. Unlike the process of reforming many economic institutions, such as trade unions or major trade laws, changing formal political institutions often means that politicians are the primary actors in the redesign of rules that are to govern their own behavior. This, of course, means that they may be motivated to steer the reform process toward institutional arrangements that are particularly favorable to their own interests. In short, the incentives for politicians under the various electoral and party system arrangements that are embedded in both the old institutional order and the possible new orders can influence the task of seeking a consensus on the direction of institutional reform.[5]

Unlike in chapter 4, I am less interested here in trying to identify tight lines of causality. My concern is more to map the cases in which we do and do not see major institutional reengineering undertaken and then to reflect on the aggregate pattern of institutional change that emerges across the four countries. The analytical focus is, ultimately, on the extent to which we see alterations in the national political architectures of these countries, and the direction of insti-

4. Ikenberry (1988, 2340). See also Krasner (1984); Collier and Collier (1991); Haggard and Kaufman (1995).
5. See for example, Geddes (1995); Shugart (1998); Haggard and Kaufman (1995); Grindle (2000); Shugart and Wattenberg (2001b); Smith and Remington (2001).

tutional change—what this does to their location on the concentra-tion-of-power range. In terms of causality, there are a mix of factors at work, including the fundamental force of shifting vectors of social coalitions, the impact of sharp exogenous shocks, and the effects of the institutional status quo itself in mediating these forces.

To varying degrees Thailand, the Philippines, Malaysia, and In-donesia were all potential candidates for institutional reform. In broad terms, the tremendous economic transformation in much of Southeast Asia during the last quarter of the twentieth century made it a likely territory for political change. Rapid industrialization stim-ulated the creation of new and broader economic elites as well as the formation of urban middle and working classes. And as underlying social formations shifted, the coalition of interests that lay behind the entrenchment of the existing configurations of political institutions weakened, and the demand for change among nascent coalitions grew. By the late twentieth century, there was a growing demand for better governance, and this implied a growing demand for in-stitutional reform. In addition to experiencing these long-term so-cioeconomic forces and their attendant implications, Thailand, the Philippines, Malaysia, and Indonesia suffered a radical economic in-terruption at the close of the twentieth century, the regional eco-nomic crisis of 1997–98. This brought the shifting vector of social forces and the emerging interests in institutional reform sharply into focus. In opposition to these factors, the extent of the dispersal of na-tional decision-making power constrained efforts to dislodge the ex-isting institutional framework and establish a new one.

Remarkable political events unfolded in these four countries in the wake of this great economic boom and bust. We see two cases of major institutional reengineering—one in which it is seriously con-templated but defeated and one in which there are some important stirrings that are insufficient to bring about political change. The sto-ries of causality are complex and varied, but the outcomes were not random. Notwithstanding the existence of important country-spe-cific nuances and contingencies, the overall pattern that emerged at the end of this episode of upheaval can be linked back strongly to the implications for governance of the distribution of decision-making power.

THAILAND

The institutional framework of Thai politics underwent major surgery in 1997 with the adoption of a new constitution that had far-reaching consequences. This is a rich and complex story. Public pressure for the reform of the country's political architecture had been building since the early 1990s as governance problems accumulated, but came to a dramatic climax with the explosion of the 1997–98 regional economic crisis. Notwithstanding the pressures for institutional reform, the obstacles to change were formidable. The country's existing political architecture was itself a major obstacle to reform. As we have seen already, Thailand's multiparty parliamentary framework made any change requiring parliamentary approval very difficult, even if it enjoyed strong support. There were very few parliamentarians who were keen to see major constitutional reform. Indeed, it was not until the task of designing a new constitution was handed to an independent commission that things began to really move ahead, and even then it required the searing discipline of a profound economic crisis to overcome parliamentary resistance.

Perhaps the best place to begin is with the loose coalition for reform that had been building through the 1990s. In broad terms, this coalition comprised two basic strands. One was concerned primarily with effective governance and was built on fears that the existing political architecture was dooming the country to perpetual policy paralysis, weak and unstable governments, and pervasive money politics. The other was more concerned with just governance—issues of democracy, human rights, and social justice. In part this was a reaction to the coup and military-inspired constitution of 1991, and in part it was a reflection of concerns that big economic interests were capturing the political process. The amalgam of groups and interests that coalesced in pushing for an overhaul of the country's political architecture ultimately stretched from moderately conservative members of the political elite to radical grassroots organizations.

Concerns about effective governance in Thailand centered on the issues of political corruption and policy paralysis. The former included problems such as business interests buying policy concessions from ministers and bureaucrats, politicians buying ministerial party leadership posts from their party and factional colleagues, and politicians and their key local backers buying votes from constituents. The latter centered on the systemic difficulty of achieving agreement within the governing multiparty coalition on broad policy reform problems, with stasis or very minor change being the typical outcome (as detailed in chapter 4, in the discussion of the country's response to the economic crisis of 1997–98). Although certainly evident during the 1980s, these problems were partly disguised under the semidemocratic regime headed by General Prem Tinsulanond. Key areas of macroeconomic policy were largely shielded from the pressures of party politics and remained the preserve of unelected technocrats answerable to Prem. Other policy arenas, however, were ceded to the elected politicians in cabinet and were routinely subject to horsetrading.[6] Problems with the quality of governance became increasingly apparent from 1988 onward as elected politicians came to assume full control. From 1991, the Institute for Public Policy Studies—an influential think tank built around prominent reformminded members of the academic and bureaucratic establishment—became a catalyst for debate in elite circles about the efficacy of Thai governance. A series of publications in the early 1990s focused on the deterioration of policy management under the leadership of corrupt politicians.[7] As the 1990s progressed, money politics issues became increasingly conspicuous, policy problems accumulated, and successive governments proved ineffectual and short-lived.[8] Bangkok's elite and middle classes became increasingly exasperated, with even the conservative and politically reticent monarch, King Bumibol Adulyadej, expressing frustration with poor governance, complaining publicly that ministers only "talk, talk, talk, and argue, argue, argue."[9]

These were the origins of the first strand of the political reform movement. The strand concerned primarily with democracy and jus-

6. Christensen et al. (1993); Doner and Laothamatas (1994).

7. Connors (1999, 207–8). Connors provides a superb account of the evolution of the political and intellectual currents underlying the reform process.

8. This is a theme in much of the scholarly literature on Thai politics in the 1990s. See, for instance Hewison (1997); Pasuk and Baker (1998); Suchit (1996b); Ockey (1994); Anek (1996); Surin (1997); Anusorn (1998); Hicken (n.d.).

9. "Royal Reproach," *Far Eastern Economic Review,* 5 October 1995, 23.

tice came to life in the wake of the military coup of 1991 and the brutal crackdown on demonstrators during Black May in 1992. The overthrow of Chatichai Choonhavan's government by General Suchinda Kraprayoon was not initially greeted with widespread opposition because Chatichai's government was seen as thoroughly besmirched by money politics and because the caretaker government General Suchinda put in place proved remarkably able and reformist under the technocratic leadership of Anand Panyarachun. However, pro-democracy groups began to coalesce as General Suchinda and his allies began to steer a markedly less democratic constitution through the assembly that he had appointed. Among the provisions of the new 1991 constitution that students and other pro-democracy activists objected to were stipulations that ministers (including the prime minister) need not be elected members of parliament and that the Senate remain an unelected body, thus preserving it as a bastion for military and bureaucratic interests. Criticism by nascent pro-democracy groups did not prevent the junta from pushing ahead with the adoption of the revised constitution. However, when new elections were held in March 1992 under the controversial new framework and General Suchinda accepted an invitation by a coalition of parties to become the unelected prime minister, protests against the reentrenchment of military power rapidly multiplied, culminating in the bloody crackdown on protesters in May. As Michael Connors points out, the importance of the Black May violence was that it consolidated a coalition of activists from nongovernmental organizations (NGOs), universities, and labor groups committed to pursuing political reform to promote democracy and equity.[10] Interwoven with opposition to the military and to the constitution it had spawned was the conviction that the existing framework of politics was allowing business interests to hijack policy at the expense of the poor.

  Notwithstanding this remarkably broad coalition for major institutional reform, the obstacles to achieving reform were considerable. In part, this was because the interests of those concerned with democracy and justice were clearly more radical than those concerned more narrowly with more efficient governance. But more than this,

10. Connors (1999, 206); Suthy (1995).

the very process of constitutional change was difficult because it required the agreement of the parliament. In the absence of nondemocratic or extra-constitutional change, the only avenue for reform was via the formal approval of the two houses of parliament meeting jointly as the National Assembly. That is, the existing institutional framework itself governed the process of institutional reform. Complicating the problem was the fact that none of the political parties was strongly committed to major reform. Members of the appointed Senate, most notably military representatives, had obvious incentives to resist political reform. But the elected politicians in the House of Representatives had equally powerful incentives to preserve the status quo—even if they were mindful of its defects—because this was a system that they had mastered and it had brought them into office. Quite literally, it was a system in which they were directly and heavily invested. Interestingly, there was no simple pattern of parties most strongly associated with vote-buying activities (e.g., Chart Thai, Chart Pattana, or New Aspiration) doing more to set back reform. When in the government, the Democrats, the party most associated with a loosely liberal agenda, supported only very modest reform measures. And perversely, it was when Chart Thai and then New Aspiration held the prime ministership that the crucial decisions opening the way to reform were made.

An initial foray into institutional reform came in 1993 with the establishment of a parliamentary committee to explore amendments to the constitution under the leadership of Chumphon Silapa-archa (brother of Banharn Silapa-archa, the leader of the opposition Chart Thai party). Although the committee produced an extensive set of recommendations for reform, the government of the day, built around Chuan Leekpai and the Democrat party, was reluctant to contemplate major change. And resistance from both the appointed Senate and opposition parties in the House thwarted the possibility of even modest changes.[11] Meanwhile, spurred on by the parliamentary impasse, the popular reform movement began to gather momentum. In May 1994 Chalard Worachart, a political activist

11. For details of these machinations, see "Anti-Reform Club," *Far Eastern Economic Review,* 12 May 1994, 17; "Disloyal Opposition," *Far Eastern Economic Review,* 14 April 1994, 16–17.

whose hunger strikes in 1992 had become a focal point for opposition to Suchinda, began a public fast to support calls for a new and more democratic constitution. In response to sharply rising public pressures, the Speaker of the House of Representatives set up a broad-based public commission, the Democratic Development Committee (DDC), chaired by the respected physician Dr. Prawase Wasi, to advise on constitutional reform. As 1994 progressed, Chuan's government debated various possible constitutional amendments arising from the earlier committee report.

Strong public support now existed for political reform, but the existing institutional configuration continued to exert is powerful antichange bias. By the end of the year, agreement had been reached on only a very modest set of constitutional amendments. The ruling coalition was torn among the contending interests of its half-dozen constituent parties. The Palang Dharma party, for instance, favored extensive reform; the Democrats preferred cautious incrementalism; and Chavalit Yongchaiyudh's New Aspiration party was strongly opposed to the possibility of democratizing local government—and even used this as a justification for walking out of the coalition. The problem was further compounded by opposition from bureaucratic and military interests in the Senate.[12] But, recall from chapter 4 that this was a familiar pattern in Thai politics. Frustration with this chronic immobilism was, of course, central to the reform push itself, and it meant that agreement could only be reached on modest constitutional amendments being approved in January 1995.[13]

Although actual institutional change at this stage was still very modest, the succession of major reports was ratcheting up the debate, providing focused discussion of governance problems as well as possible institutional solutions. This had not been the intention of the various political leaders who had authorized them, but it was the

12. For further details, see "Constitutional Conflict: Ruling Coalition at Odds over New Charter," *Far Eastern Economic Review*, 7 July 1994, 16; "Here We Go Again: New Row Threatens Ruling Coalition," *Far Eastern Economic Review*, 15 December 1994, 16; "Marriage of Convenience," *Far Eastern Economic Review*, 22 December 1994, 14–15.

13. Inter alia, these were reducing the voting age, reducing the size of the unelected Senate to two-thirds (rather than three-quarters) of the elected House of Representatives, and creating an elected independent electoral commission.

cumulative effect. In April, after laboring for ten months, the DDC presented its report to the Speaker of the House.[14] The DDC had been appointed by the parliament as a way of defusing public pressure and so had been placed in the hands of nonparliamentarians. Party leaders soon found that they were getting much more than they had bargained for. The report was remarkably forceful, highlighting problems of governance and legitimacy, focusing on a corrupt "parliamentary dictatorship," vote buying, the overcentralization of power in Bangkok, weaknesses in the rule of the law, and the need to achieve "political stability, democracy and efficient government."[15] Unfortunately, the DDC's report was presented to the parliament in April 1995—just as Chuan's government had begun to slide into terminal disarray amid scandal and coalitional defections. Although the political turmoil meant that the report was in effect shelved, it nonetheless had several important consequences. First, both symbolically and substantively, the report represented the beginning of the joining of the moderate and more radical strands of reformers by interweaving concerns about effective governance with concerns about just governance. Second, by virtue of its breadth and specificity, it had a major effect in advancing the public debate and increasing the pressure on parliamentary leaders to be responsive.[16] Third, and most important, in institutional terms it tackled two key obstacles to far-reaching reform. One was Article 211 of the existing 1991 constitution, which permitted parliament to amend the constitution but not to replace it—and thus limiting the country to piecemeal change. The DDC report recommended that parliament amend Article 211 to allow for the adoption of an entirely new constitution. The other was the involvement of politicians at all. The report recommended that the task of drawing up a new constitution be handled by an independent commission (not the parliament), with the public (not the parliament) deciding the matter by referendum. This was a critical detail. The DDC was quite deliberately arguing that the whole matter needed to be lifted out of the hands of parliament; in short, the DDC was proposing an end-run around the parliament.

14. Democracy Development Committee (1995).
15. Prudhisan (1999, 271); Connors (1999, 210).
16. Suchit (1996a, 363).

Picking up on these currents during the ensuing election campaign of May 1995, Banharn Silapa-archa, leader of opposition party, Chart Thai, promised that he would help to open the way for political reform by pursuing the recommendations of the DDC. Skeptics viewed this as little more than an electoral ploy by a conservative party (notorious for rural vote-buying) seeking to make inroads with Bangkok's middle class. Although the more progressive Democrat party refused to make such commitments, Nam Thai and Palang Dharma, two small liberal Bangkok-based parties also picked up on this as an electoral issue. When Banharn emerged as prime minister in July, heading the new and already scandal-tainted coalition, he reaffirmed in the parliament his commitment to follow the DDC's recommendations to amend Article 211 and pursue a new constitution.

If this move surprised reformers, it dismayed his own party, many other parties, and key sections of the (unelected) Senate—all of whom were very wary of the idea, particularly the notion of taking the reform process out of the hands of the parliament.[17] In response to this opposition, Banharn quickly back-pedaled, appointing a public commission—the Political Reform Committee, again headed by his brother Sulophom—to revisit the whole issue. Although there is little evidence to suggest that Banharn, the prototypical money-based politician, had any serious interest in or commitment to political reform, his brother's committee nonetheless produced a report later that year that further advanced the cause.

The committee's recommendations were very much in keeping with the spirit of the earlier DDC report, including a reaffirmation of the need to amend Article 211. Two recommendations were to be particularly important. One was for the introduction of single-member electoral districts to reduce the incentives for vote-buying. The other was for the creation of a special commission appointed by the king comprising members of parliament (MPs), senators, academics, and other public representatives to draft a new constitution, with the draft to be presented to a joint sitting of the parliament for approval and with the king having discretion to submit it to a national refer-

17. Suchit (1996a, 363–64).

endum if a majority of MPs supported it but the joint sitting of the parliament failed to do so. The latter recommendation was an attempt to craft a compromise between two conflicting realities: most MPs and senators were deeply skeptical of constitutional reform, but without parliamentary approval constitutional reform could not progress.[18]

Banharn was anything but a natural ally of institutional reform. And yet the by-product of his pursuit of electoral advantage was his inadvertent support of pushing the cause forward. In another move that surprised even his critics, Banharn, when given the opportunity in early 1996 to reshape the composition of the Senate by selecting a new cohort of appointees, instead opted for only a moderate number of military officers and boosted the representation of academics, media figures, and business people.[19] Whatever Banharn's motives, a side-effect of this move was a Senate that was less hostile to constitutional reform.

With the Thai economy showing signs of faltering through 1996 and Banharn's government becoming engulfed in one corruption scandal after another, public pressure for action on political reform grew stronger. Notwithstanding his earlier public commitments and his having established the Political Reform Committee, Banharn was very reluctant to implement actual changes. In May, reform-oriented senators introduced a Constitution Amendment Bill providing for an independent assembly consisting of one member from each of the seventy-six provinces and twenty-three experts from academia and public administration to draft a new constitution within 240 days and for a referendum to be held if a joint sitting of the parliament failed to pass the draft. With his coalition fraying and facing severe pressures within his own party, Banharn sought to head off defections by opposing the bill and insisting that parliament control the process. Public confidence in the political system was sinking to an all-time low. As one parliamentarian put it, "We're getting close to a point where it's not just dissatisfaction with Banharn, but dissatisfaction with all politicians and the political system." Or as former caretaker

18. Suchit (1996a, 363–64).

19. "Thailand: A More Diverse Senate," *Far Eastern Economic Review,* 4 April 1996, 13.

Prime Minister Anand Panyarachun bluntly put it, "We have reached a political dead-end."[20] (Recall from chap. 4 that Thailand's economic situation was also becoming a matter of growing concern at about this time.)

By August, the scandal-plagued government appeared to be sliding toward collapse. Anticipating the government's fall and fresh elections, members of the coalition moved to distance themselves from Banharn and his party and publicly associated themselves with the popular cause of constitutional reform. Desperate to stave off the collapse of the coalition and pressed from all sides, Banharn backed down and allowed a slightly modified version of the reform initiative that provided for an independent assembly to draft a new constitution. The House and Senate were duly called together for a joint sitting as the National Assembly and agreed to pass the bill, thereby amending Article 211 of the existing constitution and paving the way for the drafting of a new one.[21]

This was not the preferred outcome of any of the major parties. They had only come to this point through a combination of tactical repositioning on the reform issue in anticipation of having to go to the polls and expectations that they would still be able to shape the outcome of the drafting process by one means or another. But although shifting their public stance on the reform question helped some of the other parties, it did not save Banharn. In September, after only fifteen months in office, his government collapsed as expected and new elections were called.

Notwithstanding the deep misgivings of the great majority of parliamentarians, driven largely by coalitional and electoral expediency, they were nevertheless opening the door inch by inch to the possibility of major reform. Following the election, in which vote-buying was widely regarded to have reached new extremes, a new government was built around Chavalit's New Aspiration party. In a remarkable replay of Banharn's performance in the campaign the year

20. Both quoted in "Who Needs Democracy?" *Far Eastern Economic Review,* 19 September 1996, 20–21.
21. Prudhisan (1999, 271); "Reform at Crossroads," *Bangkok Post,* 21 August 1996; "Still No Unanimity on Charter Writers," *Bangkok Post,* 28 August 1997; "PM Acts to Sink Rival Charter Bill," *Bangkok Post,* 30 August 1996.

before, Chavalit strongly committed himself to supporting constitutional reform in an effort to enhance his party's electoral standing, promising even to call new elections once the new constitution and any necessary enabling laws had been passed. And, like Banharn before him, in the beginning he did indeed move effectively in this direction. In December, the final selection of the members of the independent Constitutional Drafting Assembly (CDA) took place. Although the short lists for each province and the expert sectors had been popularly generated, under the terms of the compromise bill providing for the CDA parliament retained the right to make the final selection from the various short lists. Unsurprisingly, this resulted in former politicians being prominent among the ninety-nine individuals chosen for the CDA.[22]

If party leaders thought this would give them a pliant drafting assembly, they were quickly disappointed. The CDA soon established itself as both independent and internally diverse. This was reflected in its leadership: Uthai Phimchaichon (a prominent pro-democracy figure who had been imprisoned for standing against the military in the 1970s) and Anand Panyarachun (the former caretaker prime minister). Uthai was closely supported by sections of the NGO movement and Anand was the standard bearer for business and middle-class demands for more effective governance. Through the first half of 1997, the CDA undertook very wide-ranging public consultations while also hosting vigorous internal debate between advocates of the narrower goal of more effective economic governance and those concerned with a broader agenda of justice and equity. Despite the breadth of the spectrum of interests within the CDA, the final vote on the draft charter was nearly unanimous.

Among the key elements in the final version of the long and complex constitution were:

- Strengthening the parties, reducing their number, and reducing their incentives for pork-barreling and vote-buying through the adoption of a hybrid mixed-member electoral system for the House. Eighty percent of seats were to be single-member dis-

22. Ockey (1997, 314); "Constitution: Democracy Advocates Slam Govt Interference in Selection of Writers," *Bangkok Post*, 27 December 1996.

tricts and the remaining 20 percent to be filled proportionately
from party lists by those parties gaining not less than 5 percent
of the national vote in a separate, single nationwide ballot.

- Producing more stable and effective governments by requiring
that all members of the cabinet relinquish their seats in parliament (thereby discouraging coalition defections), that members
of parliament give 90 days notice of a decision to change party
(also discouraging defections), and that any vote of no-confi-
dence against the prime minister be proposed by at least 40 percent of the House and simultaneously nominate his or her
replacement.

- Strengthening civil liberties, the operation of democracy, and
the rule of law through the establishment of a range of independent agencies—a Constitutional Court, an Election Commission, a National Counter-Corruption Commission, a National
Human Rights Commission, an Ombudsmen, and Administrative Courts.

- Strengthening accountability by empowering the now fully
elected Senate to appoint and remove members of the new independent agencies and to impeach both members of the cabinet and judges.

- Devolving power from the Interior Ministry in Bangkok to local
government and democratizing local government.

This strongly reformist constitution was widely touted as the people's constitution. And, indeed, there had been an extraordinary
degree of public involvement both during the initial inputs and subsequent rounds of consultation. In all, it was estimated that some
855,000 people and more than three hundred public and private organizations had been involved in the consultative processes.[23] Given
the unusually high level of public support and legitimacy attaching
to the CDA and its draft constitution, the lengthy gestation of the reform process through the mid-1990s, the ostensible endorsement of
the sitting prime minister, and the broad and deep frustration with
the dysfunctional nature of the country's existing political architec-

23. Prudhisan (1999, 273)

ture, the adoption of the new charter might have appeared to be a foregone conclusion.

The reality was very different. Notwithstanding all of these factors, there were powerful minorities strongly opposed to the new constitution. The changes to the electoral system directly threatened the interests of MPs by undermining the electoral strategies in which they were already heavily invested (this was particularly a problem for the conservative rural-based parties in the government). The requirement that those entering the cabinet resign their parliamentary seat radically affected the value of what had been the ultimate prizes in politics—ministerships. Small parties were directly threatened by the 5 percent threshold for the party-list seats. Incumbent senators were directly threatened by the introduction of elections for Senate seats. The powerful Interior Ministry and the vast network of appointed provincial and local officials beneath it were directly threatened by the decentralization and democratization of subnational government. And even sitting judges were directly threatened by the power to be vested in the Senate to remove judges for corruption.

No sooner had the CDA completed its mission in mid-August than opposition to the proposed charter came quickly and sharply into focus. Having earlier committed himself to backing constitutional reform, Chavalit now brought his support for the charter into question. Chavalit's colleague, Interior Minister Sanoh Thientong, fiercely criticized the charter, declaring it to be pro-communist and antimonarchist. The permanent secretary of the Interior Ministry echoed Sanoh's strident criticisms. Soon after, the organization representing district and village chiefs came out in opposition as well. As parliament prepared to debate the draft charter, Sanoh promised to bus thousands of district and village officials into Bangkok to oppose the charter. And in a related move, the Village Scouts, an extreme rightwing militia that had been involved in the bloody suppression of prodemocracy demonstrators in 1976, promised to mobilize in protest if the new constitution was adopted.[24]

In normal times, the opposition of the prime minister or one or

24. Prudhisan (1999, 281–83; Economist Intelligence Unit, Thailand, 3rd Quarter 1997, p. 14).

more parties in the ruling coalition would have been sufficient to veto a bill. But recall from chapter 4 the economic context in 1997— these were not normal times. By August, Thailand was in the grips of its worst financial crisis of modern times. The currency and the stock market were plunging, investor confidence was in disarray, and the IMF had been called in for emergency assistance. Chavalit's government was widely blamed for the situation because of its inability to implement effective measures to head off the crisis of confidence. Like the earlier governments headed by Banharn, Chuan, and Chatichai, Chavalit's was beset by immobilism and corruption. In this context, adoption of the new constitution had come to be seen by both the public and the markets as a necessary condition for stabilizing and then repairing the widespread economic damage. The day after Sanoh's wild suggestion that the draft constitution was a communist plot, the stock market plunged 6 percent.[25]

On top of his own misgivings about the new constitution, Chavalit was severely constrained by the need to keep Sanoh and his faction from leaving the New Aspiration party and bringing down the government (as he had brought down Banharn's government the year before when he had walked out of Chart Thai and over to Chavalit's party). With the country sliding into economic chaos, Chavalit was gambling for very high stakes in his struggle for political survival. But with the public and the markets reacting so negatively to the effort to kill off the draft constitution, other segments of the House and the Senate began to move away from Chavalit and to declare their support for the charter. The exogenous shock of the crisis was pushing opponents to shift their position. As a leading member of the conservative Chart Thai party rationalized his party's reluctant endorsement of the charter, "There are some clauses I don't like, but because of the economy we have to accept it." Meechai Ruchapun, the president of the Senate, who played a key role in finally persuading other wary senators to support the bill, elaborated:

I changed my position because when the constitution was finished the economic crisis broke out. If we looked around we could see the peo-

25. "Bangkok: Gun-Shy," *Far Eastern Economic Review,* 4 September 1997, 68.

ple had placed their hope in the constitution. . . . if we rejected the constitution the people's hope would be exhausted and it would create a severe crisis. We knew that if the constitution passed there would be problems but they would be in the future, but if it didn't pass the problems would break out then and then country would not survive.[26]

The extraordinary sense of urgency injected into the situation by the financial crisis played a pivotal role in shifting the numbers within the two houses of parliament. With the balance moving against him, Chavalit flirted with a series of tactical ploys to stymie the charter.[27] On the eve of the parliamentary debate in early September, General Chettha Thanajaro, the army commander and leader of the military cohort in the Senate, called on Chavalit to give his unequivocal support for the new constitution.[28] With the military leadership and their supporters in the Senate, members of the coalition, and even members of his own party declaring that they would now (reluctantly) support the draft constitution, Chavalit was forced to back down and announce that he and his party would indeed give it their backing. The currency rate promptly jumped up on this announcement. When he tried yet another ploy, however, and announced that the formal vote on the draft would be delayed by fifteen days, it plunged again.[29] At this stage, business organizations were openly protesting against the government in the streets. Finally, after Chavalit's holding the constitution hostage to his survival of a censure debate in the House, on September 27 a joint sitting over-

26. The first quotation is from "People's Putsch," *Far Eastern Economic Review*, 18 September 1997, 15; the second is from Connors (1999, 219). The prospect of serious conflict was real. As Sanoh and others were rallying rural protestors to their cause (called the yellow-brigade after their yellow shirts, which invoked royal and Buddhist connections), umbrella groups such as the Campaign for Democracy and other pro-democracy activists (bedecked in green, the chosen color of the constitutional reform movement) were promising mass rallies to bring down the government if it failed to support the charter (Prudhisan 1999, 281–82).

27. "NAP Tries a New Angle to Defeat Draft," *The Nation*, 5 September 1997; "Charter Taken as 'Hostage' to Secure Two Week Respite," *The Nation*, 11 September 1997.

28. Prudhisan (1999, 281–83).

29. "Political Issues Core to the Direction of the Baht," *The Nation*, 15 September 1997.

whelmingly passed the bill, with the king promulgating it shortly thereafter.

How should this remarkable case of politicians approving far-reaching changes for which they had little real enthusiasm be interpreted? Widespread opposition from politicians threatened by institutional reform and the inherent difficulties of effecting change because of Thailand's fragmented parliamentary framework presented powerful roadblocks to would-be reformers. And then the searing heat of the national economic crisis forced the politicians into final submission. More broadly, however, the striking feature of the Thai case is the extent to which the push for reform was itself informed by the deeply dysfunctional pattern of governance inherent in the country's existing institutional framework. Concerns about policy immobilism and paralysis were a central plank of the reform push. And, of course, these concerns were catastrophically borne out by the chronic inability of parliament to respond in a timely and effective manner to the country's mounting economic problems as the 1990s progressed. And, as we see later in the comparative discussion, a primary outcome of Thailand's institutional reforms was a reduction in the fragmentation of national decision-making power.

THE PHILIPPINES

The Philippines provides a fascinating and revealing comparison with Thailand. Both countries were in the process of consolidating democratic governments in the late 1990s, with authoritarian rule looming large in their recent pasts. Concern about effective governance was a pressing issue in both cases, there being, in varying degrees, evident problems of legislative delay and gridlock. In both cases, the onset of the regional 1997–98 financial crisis coincided with institutional reform becoming a very hot political issue. And in both cases, we see politicians moving to promote or oppose ideas for changes to the national political architecture, depending on how the institutional status quo affected their interests. Yet in other respects, the dynamics and immediate outcomes were starkly different. In the

Philippine case, the push to alter the country's political architecture was defeated by a combination of focused opposition from within the legislature and, ultimately, a broadly based popular movement anxious to guard against any move in the direction of recentralizing power in the presidency. Although there were certainly concerns about effective governance in the Philippines, despite all its problems there was no broad consensus that the existing institutional framework was fundamentally flawed. Indeed, the proposed changes conjured up associations with the country's authoritarian past, creating a broad and powerful coalition to defend the existing framework.

The push for a reform of the country's political architecture in the 1990s under the Ramos administration grew out of the experiences of the previous administration of Corazon Aquino. Notwithstanding the widespread public support for the reconsolidation of democratic government under Aquino and the Freedom Constitution of 1987, serious questions about the effectiveness of the particular institutional framework that had been adopted emerged during her tenure. Particularly in light of the slow progress of policy reform, concerns about the dangers of executive-legislative deadlock and arguments in favor of a parliamentary rather than presidential form of government began to surface. This was not a new theme in Philippine politics, having been featured in different ways in the Constitutional Commission of 1987 and the Constitutional Conventions of 1971 and 1934.[30] Fidel Ramos picked up on this in the presidential election campaign, and in his June 1992 inaugural address he declared, "When the time is opportune, I also intend to ask Congress to convene itself as a constituent assembly for the purpose of amending the constitution."[31]

For a president with an activist reform agenda, the prospect of legislative frustration at the hands of one or both houses of congress was a matter of fundamental concern. If the Philippines was to shake off its reputation as the economic sick man of Southeast Asia and attract new investment, there were countless long-standing policy problems

30. Santos (1997) reviews the long history of debates about constitutional reform in the Philippines.

31. Quoted in Florentino-Hofilena (1997, 148).

that required remedial action. A political framework in which decision making was less fragmented would, it was argued, greatly facilitate the task of tackling the country's enormous developmental challenges.[32] In October 1993, the House unanimously passed a resolution calling for both chambers of congress to convene as a constituent assembly to enable a constitutional shift to a form of parliamentary government, possibly modeled on France's hybrid system.[33] Although the idea was promoted by Ramos and his close ally House Speaker, Jose de Venecia, it was fiercely opposed by the Senate. That many senators took this position was scarcely surprising; the Senate stood to be abolished under the proposal.[34] Senate opposition to a shift to parliamentarism was the most conspicuous obstacle to institutional change, but it was by no means the only one. More subtle, but no less inimical, to the emergence of a strong pro-change coalition was the fact that Ramos turned out to be remarkably successful in securing congressional cooperation with his legislative agenda. Although congressional cooperation for economic reform was piecemeal and came at a high price—a very extensive and well-oiled system of pork barreling and legislative patronage—it was attainable.[35] Ironically, then, although he was at the front of the campaign to restructure the country's political architecture in the name of more efficient governance, Ramos himself demonstrated that far-reaching policy reform was indeed possible under the existing institutional framework.[36] The system of governance was by no means pretty, but it was tolerably effective, as seen in the Philippine response to the Asian economic crisis described in chapter 4.

From about the middle of 1995, the debate began to shift as serious attention was focused on the possibility of constitutional restructuring. But, as became increasingly apparent, this had less to do

32. Florencio Abad (1997), a member of the House of Representatives, makes the case for institutional reform to overcome problems of legislative gridlock.

33. Abad (1997, 48); "Going Solo: Return to Single-Chamber Legislature Mooted," *Far Eastern Economic Review,* 3 June 1993, 22.

34. On legislative pork under Ramos, see Bolongaita (1995, 106).

35. Coronel (1998); de Dios (1999).

36. For an overview and discussion of the sweeping economic policy changes that Ramos introduced, see Timberman (1998).

with the supposed benefits of any particular institutional form of government than it did with political tenure and electoral advantage. The year 1995 marked the midpoint of Ramos's tenure. He had only three years left before the constitutional term limit forced him into political retirement. The president was not the only player with term-limit worries. Term limits for the Senate and House meant that come the next national elections in May 1998, along with Ramos approximately one-third of all senators and one-half of all representatives would also be barred from running. For a politician staring at political mortality, a parliamentary framework—in which there were no term limits—held evident appeal. But just as incentives to politicians under the existing framework motivated many to support institutional reform, so too did they motivate others to defend the status quo. Senators not yet confronting a term limit were unlikely to support moves to abolish their own chamber. And further, with the Senate serving as the traditional breeding ground for presidential contenders, a substantial number of senators harbored well-developed ambitions to contest the presidency in 1998. This, of course, made them even less likely to support a constitutional shift away from presidentialism at that time.

The push for parliamentarism produced intense political maneuvering. In August 1995, the House Committee on Constitutional Amendments began public hearings on parliamentarism and constitutional change. At the end of the same month, the Senate president, Edgardo Angara, was toppled from his leadership post in a move that was widely seen to have been engineered by Ramos's aides. Angara, an apparently strong contender for the presidency in the next election, had indicated he was supportive of constitutional reform, but not until after the 1998 election. This, of course, would be too late for Ramos and his team. In early September, the *Manila Times* published a leaked draft parliamentary constitution, apparently prepared by the National Security Council (headed by Ramos's principal political strategist, Jose Almonte). The leaked document stirred up a great controversy not simply because it suggested that the government's plans for a parliamentary framework were well advanced, but, more important, because the draft was remarkable for its extraordinarily attenuated mechanisms for executive accountability to the parliament.[37] In view of the well-recognized preference of Ramos and Almonte for strong and decisive government, Ramos's own involvement in the Marcos regime, and the unfortunate parallels between the constitutional changes mooted now and those which Marcos had used as a precursor to naked authoritarianism, it was scarcely surprising that public distrust very rapidly spread. Senate opponents to the plan were soon joined by Corazon Aquino, the former president; Manila Archbishop Jaime Sin, and a range of social and political organizations.[38]

In the face of this opposition, by early 1996 the whole notion of radical constitutional surgery and a shift to parliamentary government was effectively shelved. The push for institutional change did not, however, die. Although Ramos's public position continued to be that he expected to leave office in 1998, his aides and supporters were focusing on a new strategy: instead of changing the entire structure of government, they would seek a constitutional amendment to provide for a two-term rather than one-term limit. With systemic arguments about efficient governance now abandoned, what remained was the self-interest of the Ramos team in forestalling political mortality and the wider interest of Ramos's supporters in extending his tenure for fear that his successor would be unable to maintain the pro-development policy crusade. This fear was heightened by polls that consistently showed that the front-runner for the presidency in 1998 was Joseph Estrada, who was seen in elite circles as an amateurish policy lightweight brandishing populist slogans. The terms of the debate were thus now quite different: an argument for amending the constitution in the hope that the next six years would also be characterized by effective governance and a generally pro-development policy environment versus an argument that changing the country's fundamental political rules merely to accommodate an individual president jeopardized the achievements of the previous decade by undermining the democratic foundations on which they rested.

37. *Manila Times*, 5–6 September 1995. Among other things, there was no provision for a vote of no confidence in the prime minister or parliamentary question time, and checks on the terms for a declaration of martial law were markedly diluted. See Florentino-Hofilena (1997, 144).

38. Florentino-Hofilena (1997, 144–45).

The tactics of Ramos's supporters shifted as well. Rather than attempting to pursue constitutional change through the congress, the plan was to use the untested people's initiative provision of the 1987 constitution, under which a referendum on a constitutional change might be triggered if a petition was signed by at least 3 percent of voters in each of the 204 congressional districts and 12 percent of voters nationwide. In late 1996, a private organization, PIRMA (People's Initiative for Reform, Modernization, and Action; *pirma* means sign) began rapidly collecting signatures on Ramos's behalf. In this they were helped by his now-substantial track record: four years of increasingly robust economic growth together with the successful 1996 Manila APEC (Asia Pacific Economic Cooperation) summit, which produced ringing international endorsement of Ramos's achievements.

But even as the movement was gathering momentum, opponents were moving to head it off. In February 1997, the Senate made its view clear by passing a resolution declaring that any amendment to the term-limits provision should not be enacted until after the upcoming 1998 limit had taken effect. In March, Senator Miriam Defensor Santiago, an implacable Ramos foe, filed suit with the Supreme Court challenging the validity of the people's initiative strategy for amending the constitution. The court issued a restraining order halting the process on the grounds that this mechanism was inadequate for the purposes of amending the constitution (as distinct from lesser laws).[39]

With time very rapidly running out, Ramos's supporters moved into high gear. The Supreme Court's decision was challenged on appeal and, although upheld in June, the margin of the judicial majority was very much narrower. And when the court decided to entertain yet another appeal in late July, it appeared increasingly ambivalent, inviting speculation that it might be contemplating reversing itself. Simultaneously, Ramos's supporters opened another front by attempting to have both houses of congress convene as a constituent assembly, with the aim being to swamp any Senate opposition to constitutional change with the vastly more numerous House.[40] In

39. Magno (1998, 209).
40. "Let the Games Begin," *Far Eastern Economic Review,* 28 August 1997, 24–26.

support of this goal, in August the House Rules Committee voted to consider Resolution 40, which called for congress to convene as a constituent assembly and vote on the proposed constitutional amendments.

In this increasingly frenzied political climate, the Asian financial crisis hit the Philippines. Following the floating of the Thai baht on July 2 and the end of Manila's attempt to defend the peso on July 11, the currency fell sharply through July, August, and September. At this stage, reform of political institutions was indeed on the table in both Thailand and the Philippines, but the circumstances in the two countries were radically different. In Thailand the crisis struck a country crying out for constitutional reform, in which the political system was demonstrably failing to deliver the policy goods; in the Philippines the crisis struck a country that had just come through an unprecedented reform era and, whatever the alleged defects of its political framework when compared to some parliamentary ideal, the political framework was not demonstrably failing. This had important consequences; unlike the Thai situation, far from there being widespread public support for the mooted constitutional change, there was in fact widespread hostility to what was seen as at best a self-serving and disruptive political ploy, with eerie parallels to the prelude of the Marcos dictatorship.

It mattered little that Ramos had stood with Aquino against Marcos during the dying days of his dictatorship, that he had stood with her in defending constitutional government against repeated coup attempts by the military during her presidency, or that he had delivered a stunning economic turnaround during his own presidency. By this stage, the more salient facts were that he was a cousin of Marcos, that he had served as head of the Philippine constabulary under Marcos, and that he was now proposing to meddle with the country's democratic framework—a framework that had only recently been resurrected and that was not obviously failing. The old anti-Marcos people's power coalition of the late 1980s rapidly remobilized against the constitutional change campaign. Aquino and Cardinal Sin called for a massive protest against the campaign and scheduled it for September 21—the twenty-fifth anniversary of Marcos's declaration of martial law. But not only was the anti-charter-change movement getting larger, its composition was also broadening as business interests became increasingly doubtful of the benefits of amending the constitution. In Thailand, the financial crisis had the effect of encouraging business to rally in support of institutional change; in the Philippines, it had the opposite effect. With the stock market and the peso plunging, business groups that had been close supporters of Ramos began to back away from him rapidly. Any conceivable policy gains of prolonging Ramos's time in office were now outweighed by the prospect of immediate social conflict over the constitutional amendment and undermining the most important developmental achievement of the previous decade—a stable and workable democratic framework of government.

In September, the country's four leading business associations released a joint statement opposing any move to amend the constitution, arguing that it would only destabilize the economy and deter investment. The last time the business associations had published such a strong joint statement was in calling for Marcos to step down in 1984.[41] Although appreciating Ramos's reform record and fearing the prospect of an Estrada administration, investors evidently placed an even higher value on preserving the existing institutional framework of government. Recognizing the scale of the opposition movement that had now come together, the day before the scheduled mass rally Ramos issued an unambiguous statement declaring that he would not be a candidate in 1998 and that, although he still believed in the need for constitutional reform, any such changes would not take place until after the 1998 elections.

As in Thailand, the reform of political institutions had a history stretching back several years and became a fiercely contested issue when the financial crisis stuck. But unlike in Thailand, in the Philippines the institutional status quo was preserved. Several factors account for this. First, whatever its weaknesses, the Philippine political framework was not grossly dysfunctional.[42] Far from failing to pro-

41. "Crisis Compounded," *Far Eastern Economic Review*, 18 August 1997, 24.

42. For discussions of problems with weak parties, an overpowerful presidency, and rampant pork-barrel politics, see Velasco (1999), Leones and Moraleda (1998), Kasuya (1999), de Dios (1999), Coronel (1998), Montinola (1999), and Hutchcroft (1999).

duce policy reform, under Ramos it had done the opposite. This is an important reason why there was no broad-based movement in support of change to the country's basic political rules. Second, the campaign to change term limits that ultimately emerged appeared to offer few public benefits. Indeed, rather than the public pressing leading politicians to implement widely sought constitutional changes, this was a case of the public pressing leading politicians not to fiddle with the system. And third, given these conditions, when the financial crisis struck, it encouraged the private sector to defend the status quo.

More broadly, in the Philippines the existing political architecture was prone to neither of the deeply problematic policy syndromes we have considered—policy rigidity, associated with severely centralized decision-making power, and policy volatility, associated with severely fragmented decision-making power. Whatever the imperfections of the institutional status quo, the prevailing view was that it was worth defending in the face of a campaign for change that conjured up images of a possible return to a radically centralized power structure.

MALAYSIA

Malaysia presents an interesting case of the dog that did not bark. Alone among the four countries, it did not wrestle seriously with the possibility of adjusting its basic political institutions in the wake of the turmoil unleashed by the 1997–98 financial crisis. Certainly Malaysia experienced a severe economic shock in 1997–98 that triggered intense struggle and placed the political system under severe strain. The crisis brought a leadership battle between the prime minister and his deputy to a head and unleashed a wider political movement for *reformasi* that placed governance questions at the center of national debate and spilled over into the general election of 1999. Yet the country's highly centralized political architecture emerged largely unscathed. A concerted push for change was not thwarted by some exogenous or highly contingent factor nor was there was a powerful sense that Malaysia's political architecture was so satisfactory that there was no need for reform. Clearly, there was a constituency for a less-centralized political framework, but its voice was muted or diluted by cross-cutting sets of preferences. There is an intriguing irony in this case, for although Malaysia moved least in contemplating change to its political architecture, it is in fact remarkably susceptible to such change. Institutional constraints are not a primary obstacle to the dislodgement of the country's existing political framework. As we show later, relatively modest shifts in the dynamics of Malaysia's party system could easily produce major changes in the configuration of decision-making power.

Unlike the Thai and Philippine cases, the financial crisis did not strike in a context in which there was a well-developed campaign for or even debate about altering the country's political architecture. Instead, it struck in a context of a long-simmering leadership struggle within UMNO, the dominant component party within the wider ruling party formation, Barisan Nasional. Although ostensibly Mahathir's protégé, Anwar Ibrahim's rapid rise to the deputy prime ministership and the deputy presidency of UMNO had seen him emerge as a potential threat to Mahathir's grip on the party leadership and thus the government. The economic crisis was the catalyst that brought the rivalry to a head, with the two men differing fundamentally in their approaches to the policy management of the crisis. Mahathir's rhetoric and unorthodox policy approach to the unfolding crisis in the second half of 1997 were widely seen to have exacerbated the situation, with his every utterance seeming to drive down the value of the ringgit and the stock market. In pushing for economic reform and highlighting areas of cronyism, Anwar effectively called into question Mahathir's stewardship of the country. For the brief period in the first quarter of 1998 when he was allowed policy leadership, Anwar's more orthodox remedies, although popular internationally, imposed heavy costs on the local corporate sector. In the time leading up to the annual UMNO General Assembly in June 1998, Anwar and his supporters began openly assailing Mahathir and likening him to Suharto in Indonesia. As Anwar baldly put it, "If we are unwilling to accept [political reform], we may face the Indonesian situation where people demanded changes."[43]

Mahathir's counterstrike was swift and lethal. At the party General

43. Quoted in Felker (1999, 44).

Assembly, he regained the political initiative by releasing a detailed list of government projects that made it clear that many of Anwar's associates were also the beneficiaries of public largesse. He then moved to force the resignation of a series of Anwar supporters before ultimately firing Anwar from the cabinet and having him expelled from the party by a unanimous vote of the UMNO Supreme Council. Anwar succeeded in mobilizing significant public support, with mass rallies and an unprecedented gathering on September 20 of 30,000 protesters to hear him speak from the National Mosque and then march to Mahathir's residence to call for his ouster. Kuala Lumpur witnessed extraordinary scenes as police clashed violently with protesters. Anwar was arrested the same evening and many of his key aides met a similar fate in the following weeks.[44]

The economic turmoil of 1997–98, Anwar's attempt to stand against Mahathir, and Mahathir's draconian moves to crush Anwar—epitomized by pictures of Anwar in police detention with a blackened eye—had a powerful catalytic effect on Malaysian politics. Complaints about democratic abuses were nothing new in Malaysia, but now governance became the focal issue. And Anwar, who had been very much a part of the UMNO establishment, now became the symbol for political change. Just before his arrest Anwar called for a *reformasi* campaign—a plea that tapped a strong current of concern among disaffected Malaysians and triggered a burgeoning social movement building around a loose coalition of NGOs, Internet sites, and opposition political parties (including a new party, Keadilan, centered around Anwar's wife, Dr. Wan Azizah Ismail). Throughout 1999, the key political parties gathered under the *reformasi* banner were able to fashion an alliance of sorts, presenting an unusually united front against the government. The broad *reformasi* coalition hammered hard on themes such as Mahathir's cruel and arbitrary rule, the weakness of parliament and the judiciary, the manipulation of the press and the Electoral Commission, and the existence of widespread cronyism and corruption.[45] Interestingly, notwithstanding the heavy emphasis on the sorts of governance problems that we as-

44. Felker (1999, 45).
45. Khoo (2000, 171–75); Funston (1999, 72–73; 2000, 36–43); Weiss (2000, 420–25).

sociate with a heavily centralized semidemocratic political framework, relatively little attention was given to the institutional factors that underlay them. The patchwork coalition of opposition parties agreed to blame Mahathir and his party, but questions about how they themselves might organize political life were too divisive and left well alone.

The government's response to these extraordinary developments was revealing. In terms of campaign rhetoric, it argued that the opposition parties threatened the country's established formula for ethnic cooperation and national stability. In this, it was playing to the fears of both the Malay majority and non-Malay minorities (especially the large Chinese community). Organizationally, Mahathir moved to revise the UMNO constitution to attenuate party control of the leadership by postponing internal elections for leadership posts by up to eighteen months and raising the barriers to any would-be contestants for these posts.[46] At the very time the opposition parties were targeting the country's heavily centralized political framework, Mahathir was pushing even further toward centralization by altering the rules to strengthen his position still more. And whatever its misgivings, UMNO acquiesced to these changes. In short, the government's approach was to tighten its own internal operations to minimize dissent and to play on primordial cleavages by emphasizing the traditional themes of ethnic cohabitation and progress.

The economic crisis and the political struggle it triggered had shaken the country's political system and placed elemental questions about governance squarely in the spotlight. Yet when matters came to a head in the general election of November 1999, the country's political framework and pattern of governance emerged essentially unchanged. Certainly the election produced some important partisan shifts. Although Barisan won 148 of the 193 seats in the House of Representatives, this was less than an effective total of 169 seats in the previous parliament. More pointedly, UMNO saw its seat total fall sharply from 94 to 72, and for the first time its total did not exceed the sum of all other seats held by Barisan members. The results were a stark rebuff for Mahathir and UMNO and reflected widespread

46. Funston (2000, 31, 57).

abhorrence of Mahathir's draconian treatment of Anwar and his supporters.[47] Yet, even allowing for the well-known inequities in Malaysia's electoral competition—taken to new heights this time with the refusal to allow some 680,000 newly registered young voters to participate—the electoral results did not signal a powerful demand for changing the political framework. No doubt dirty tricks during the polling succeeded in muting the pro-reform vote, making it difficult, as Meredith Weiss rightly notes, to draw a precise meaning from Malaysia's elections, but some basic implications do come through.[48] As William Case has pointed out, disaffected Malays who had previously voted for UMNO candidates shifted not to the new pan-ethnic progressive party Keadilan (headed by Anwar's wife) or even its most prominent liberal reform candidates, but to Partai Islam Se-Malaysia (PAS), a conspicuously Malay-based rural Islamic party.[49] Conversely, the non-Malay component parties within Barisan held their ground reasonably well. In other words, no matter how disenchanted, the ethnic minorities—most notably the Chinese Malaysians—were simply unwilling to risk destabilizing the country's ethnic balance and preferred to stay within Barisan. Notwithstanding the rapid growth of a coalition focused on reform, the traditional ethnic concerns of many Malaysian voters continued to be exerted, evidently carrying more weight than any concerns about governance and the centralization of power.[50] Indeed, it is notable that not even the *reformasi* coalition pushed to overturn the gerrymandering that weighted the country's electoral system heavily in favor of Malays.

Malaysia presents us with a subtle and intriguing case of potential change that did not happen, despite the existence of short- and long-term factors that might lead us to expect otherwise. The risks of arbitrary and even capricious governance that were embedded in

47. "Election Post-Mortem: UMNO's Malay Dilemma," *Sunday Times* (Kuala Lumpur), 5 December 1999; Funston (2000).

48. Weiss (2000, 425–35).

49. Case (2001).

50. This is a central and enduring theme in the literature on Malaysian politics. Jesudason (1999) provides a particularly good analysis of the influence of ethnic factors on Malaysia's party system. More broadly, see Crouch (1996), Jesudason (1989), Gomez (1998) and Milne and Mauzy (1999).

Malaysia's political architecture had been made very clear by the government's handling of the financial crisis and, subsequently, in the treatment of Anwar and his supporters. Governance concerns of this sort were not new in Malaysia—the centralized political architecture had been in place for some time—but such concerns were brought into much sharper relief by 1998. Although the turmoil of 1997–98 did indeed generate broad and deep public anxiety and provide the catalyst for the formation of a reformist political coalition focused on problems of autocratic and arbitrary governance, this did not lead to any major modification of the country's basic political architecture; concerns about autocratic and arbitrary governance under a political framework of strongly centralized power were factored with concerns about the preservation of core ethnic interests, which took precedence over the quality of governance.

Finally, it is worth noting that although this episode suggests that Malaysia's political architecture was highly durable, this is deceptive; the character of its party system in fact made it very susceptible to change. The heavy concentration of decision-making power in Malaysia could be reversed very easily—without any alteration to the country's basic political rules. Recall that the heavy centralization of decision making was in part dependent on a set of delegation relationships that were, in large measure, voluntary in nature: the other component parties in Barisan were willing to delegate much of their authority to UMNO and the UMNO rank-and-file were willing to delegate much of its authority to its party leadership. If UMNO members became less willing to accede to the prime minister's desire to seriously limit competition for leadership posts, the collective nature of the single veto player would be strengthened greatly. This would be a significant qualitative shift. More dramatically, if the minor parties in Barisan were to behave in a more independent fashion—more like members of a genuine coalition, as opposed to merely components of a de facto single party—the dynamics of government would change markedly. In short, if the minor parties were willing to risk defection from the government, they would become separate veto players, more akin to their Thai counterparts, thereby shifting the configuration of power fundamentally.

Interestingly, there has been in fact some modest signs of activity in this direction in the wake of the 1999 election. Although Mahathir did succeed in inducing party members to accede to his demand that neither he nor his new deputy face challengers at the General Assembly in May 2000, there was very considerable disquiet about this within the party and his deputy came close to facing formal competition.[51] Separately, there have also been some signs of stirring among minority parties in Barisan. The 1999 election was the first time that UMNO's total did not exceed the combined sum of seats held by all other Barisan members. The implications of this were not lost on the MCA, which played an important role in preserving Barisan's overall parliamentary dominance. In the wake of the election, the MCA pushed for a substantial increase in the number of ministerial posts awarded to it within the government. Desperate to avoid weakening his own position within UMNO further by taking away important posts from senior party figures, Mahathir refused. Although the MCA did indeed back down, the episode brings clearly into focus the potential for change if smaller ethnic and regional parties within Barisan become more assertive.[52] Both of these modest developments may amount to nothing more, but they do help to illuminate the surprising potential for change in this long-standing political framework.

INDONESIA

Indonesia once again presents the extreme case, with its political architecture undergoing dramatic change in the wake of the 1997–98 regional financial crisis. The changes to Indonesia's political architecture were so fundamental that it was a case of regime shift—entrenched authoritarian rule was replaced by a shaky new democracy. Like the Thai case, Indonesia's experience with institutional change was complex and multidimensional. We have already seen that the extreme configuration of decision-making power embedded in the country's political architecture contributed powerfully to the

51. See "UMNO's Dilemma," *Far Eastern Economic Review,* 2 March 2000, 18–19.
52. For details on the episode, see "Storm Warning," *Far Eastern Economic Review,* 1 June 2000, 22.

economic disaster of 1997–98. But this fed back on itself, the economic disaster in turn playing a crucial role in triggering political change. Indonesia provides the clearest example among our cases of a major exogenous shock opening the door to institutional change. The radical economic reversal undermined Suharto's position, fracturing the coalition he had headed for so many years and triggering massive public protest. Moreover, once Suharto had departed and the old regime had collapsed, institutional reform became inevitable. It was not a question of whether to change the rules or not but rather in which specific ways the rules were to be changed. And there was a remarkable level of tacit agreement on the overall direction of reform: scaling back the power of the executive branch, freeing up the political parties, and boosting the legislature. When it came to the details of institutional design, we see the politicians largely controlling the process, pushing very purposefully to advance particular design features that would be advantageous to them. And more broadly, there was widespread agreement about institutional features that had failed the country in the past and that were to be avoided as it grappled with the task of institutional redesign.

Unlike Thailand and the Philippines, there had been no extensive consideration of altering the institutional configuration of politics prior to Suharto's fall. Suharto himself was not interested in significant change, and the highly centralized nature of the regime meant that he was able to impose his preferences. Throughout the early 1990s, however, there were signs of mounting frustration with his long-running rule. This prompted Suharto to make some small, low-cost concessions. In 1995, in a largely symbolic gesture that had as much to do with keeping the army in line as appeasing popular desire for reform, Suharto ordered the reduction in the number of seats allocated to the armed forces in the House of Representatives (from 20 to 15 percent). Separately, and prior to this move, he had commissioned a report on political reform from the Indonesian Institute of Science. The report turned out to be unusually substantive—so much so that the government would not allow it to be released. The main thrust of the new report was that power should be decentralized by strengthening the independence of the legislature so that it might become something more than a rubber stamp.

The report proposed lifting restrictions on the number of political parties, eliminating entirely military seats in the House of Representatives, introducing a two-term (five-years each) limit on the presidency, modifying the electoral framework to combine elements of a district system with the existing proportional representation system, and requiring House members to be actual residents of the area they represented. Significantly, it was also recommended that these reforms be implemented gradually over a ten-year period between 1997 and 2007. In closed-door discussions in 1996, a number of senior military and political officials endorsed the gradual implementation of these changes in principle. Unsurprisingly, however, in practice the initiative went nowhere. Suharto declared simply that "it wasn't yet time," and the matter was closed.[53]

That senior members of the government would endorse such ideas even in principle, was a small indication of the growing—if largely hidden—demand within the elite for institutional reform. Some sense of the mounting popular frustration with Suharto's long-running regime came in mid-1996 when the government contrived to have the Indonesian Democracy Party (PDI) reverse its decision to elect the popular opposition figure, Megawati Sukarnoputri, as its leader and then used hired thugs to eject her supporters from the party's premises. In a rapidly escalating popular backlash in July, Jakarta witnessed its most violent demonstrations in more than twenty years.

But with sustained prosperity continuing to roll and a highly centralized political structure with an effective framework of military control in place, there was little scope for change.[54] There was a marked increase in local riots and instances of civil disturbance across the country through 1996 and 1997, but there was nothing approaching a coherent or organized challenge to the government that might force change. Although more violent than usual, the general election of May 1997 produced an embarrassingly large landslide victory for the ruling party, Golongan Karya (GOLKAR).[55] In

53. Quoted in "Into the Void," *Far Eastern Economic Review*, 4 June 1998, 18.

54. For analyses of the institutional dynamics of Suharto's regime, see Surbakti (1999), Juoro (1998), and MacIntyre (1999b).

55. Sukma (1998, 106–11).

spite of the mounting dissatisfaction, Suharto and the political frame-work he had created were still secure. It took the stunning economic collapse in the final months of 1997 and the beginning of 1998 to crack the coalition and ultimately the regime. The devastating eco-nomic reversal—which saw both humble householders and giant cor-porations abandon the national currency—stripped the government of its legitimacy-enhancing claim to economic success and pushed much of the political elite and the broader middle class to join the stu-dents and urban poor in seeking an end to Suharto's regime.

The twin shocks of radical economic reversal and then regime col-lapse were essential for opening the door to institutional reform. Prior to these shocks—indeed, as late as October 1997—it was very hard to imagine that major reform might be imminent. But upon Suharto's fall, institutional restructuring became all but inevitable. Even if his successor, B. J. Habibie, had been so motivated, it was ap-parent to all that he could not sustain the old framework. Indeed, un-der Habibie it became so clear that a major change was coming that a tacit consensus quickly emerged among the principal players to hang onto the existing 1945 constitution so that it might serve as a sort of mooring at a time when so much else was adrift in a sea of change. Rather than throw out the deeply deficient constitution, the president, the military, the heads of the major parties, and much of the media agreed that it should become the foundation from which reform would proceed.[56] This had important consequences. It meant that the House of Representatives together with the ultimate politi-cal authority, the People's Consultative Assembly (comprising the House plus appointed regional and social representatives) would control the process of institutional reform. As in Thailand, there was a broad (although recent) coalition in favor of reform, but, unlike Thailand, there was no delegation of authority to an independent body and little scope for public consultation. Far from tying their own hands, the politicians themselves directly controled the redesign process. This produced ambiguous results. During the first phase of political reform (mid-1998 to mid-1999), it worked surprisingly well. Subsequently, however, this became increasingly problematic.

56. Liddle (2001).

Shortly after assuming the presidency in May 1998, Habibie took a series of steps that set the formal processes of institutional change in motion. Severely compromised by his past close association with Suharto and with a very uncertain grip on the presidency, he sought to stay abreast of the massive public pressures for rapid reform. He began by declaring that new elections for the House of Representatives would be held in May 1999 and then that a new and democratically constituted Consultative Assembly would choose a president and vice president in December. In a series of rapid reforms, he also ordered the unshackling of the press, the release of political prisoners, and the overturning of laws that permitted only three parties to exist.[57] The lifting of Suharto-era controls on political parties transformed national politics more than any other single institutional change. Once parties were able to take on a life of their own, the dynamics of the political system changed fundamentally. Having lifted the old legal controls, new rules were needed to provide the framework for democracy to begin to function. Three new basic laws—covering political parties, elections, and membership in the House and the Assembly—were passed by January 1999 to pave the way for a House election in May and the subsequent selection of a president by the Assembly.

The proposed basic laws did not represent changes to the constitution as such, but they did replace a series of laws and executive decrees from the Suharto era that had provided for such a heavily centralized and undemocratic political framework.[58] In essence, these three basic political laws reconfigured the lines of political accountability in Indonesia—that is the relationship between voters and politicians and the relationships among the various organs of the state, the executive branch (principally the president as chief executive, but also the military), the House of Representatives, and the Consultative Assembly.

The House of Representatives was primarily responsible for the three new basic laws, with most of the initial debate being handled

57. Crouch (2000); "Getting on With It," *Far Eastern Economic Review*, 25 June 1998, 20–21.
58. The constitution itself is a very brief and vague document; many important political rules are laid down in subsidiary laws.

through an eighty-seven-member Special Commission comprising members of the three parties that had contested the 1997 election together with members of the military's appointed parliamentary representatives. The previously suppressed report that Suharto had commissioned from the Indonesian Institute of Science provided an early point of reference for the House. Separately, in July Habibie appointed a small and independent team of political scientists (*Tim Tujuh*) under the leadership of Ryaas Rasyid to prepare drafts of the three basic laws.[59] After consulting widely with the existing political parties, leaders of the major new parties that had now sprung to life, and key players in the executive (notably, the president, the military, and the hierarchy of subnational bureaucracies), in August Tim Tu-juh's proposals were submitted by the government to the House as three draft bills.

The House's deliberations on the draft laws were interrupted by a Special Session of the People's Assembly in November. The Assembly was the superior body, but its public legitimacy was severely compromised at that time because more than half of its members were direct Suharto appointees and the remainder were members of the House elected under Suharto-era practices. As Vedi Hadiz has argued, the Assembly's conservative makeup and unwillingness to tackle the hard questions served to rally popular protests again to a level not seen since Suharto's fall in May and also helped to join the urban poor with the disparate student protestors.[60] The return of very large-scale popular protests was a powerful reminder that although the politicians had formal control of the reform process, ignoring the mood on the streets altogether was to invite disaster.

Ultimately, the Assembly's most significant act was issuing a decree providing for a two-term limit on the presidency. Although it did discuss broader reform questions, legislative passage of these items was left to the House. Ultimately, the House succeeded in passing the three new laws by its January 28 deadline, but only after fierce and protracted debate among the political parties, producing a number of significant modifications to the original bills. Although the in-

59. This team worked under the auspices of the Interior Ministry; another team was working under the Justice Ministry, although it proved to be less important.
60. Hadiz (1999, 111).

cumbent politicians were all hangovers from the Suharto era and its systems of managed elections, all had their eyes clearly focused on the new game of competitive elections, understanding full well that the design of the institutional framework would favor some interests over others. With the parties scrambling in anticipation of possible advantage in the coming electoral contest, the primary cleavage was between GOLKAR and the other much smaller parties. Although GOLKAR had the numbers to prevail, the smaller parties could credibly threaten to walk out of the negotiations, raising the possibility of chaos on the streets.

The bill on the electoral system had proposed a mixed electoral system (comparable to that adopted in Thailand), which combined single-member district seats with proportional representation (PR) party-list seats. After extensive debate, and partly driven by fears among the smaller parties that GOLKAR's legacy of dominance of local-level administrative agencies would give it an unfair advantage in single-member district seats, it was agreed to stick with the existing PR formula. In addition, a PR formula was very much in the interests of the smaller parties because it would produce a multiparty system.[61] More broadly, a PR-list system had appeal for the leaders of all parties because it was likely to strengthen their position vis-á-vis the party rank and file through their control of the list rankings.

The central element of the bill on political parties was the removal of government controls on the formation and activities of parties. Parties were to become formally autonomous of the government and free to organize and campaign all the way down to the village level. One major area of controversy over the bill on political parties centered on provisions in the draft that were designed to set a high barrier against very small parties. With nearly one hundred parties having been formed by late 1997 and fearing a repeat of the chaotic and debilitatingly fragmented party system in existence during the country's first encounter with democracy in the 1950s, Tim Tujuh proposed that parties seeking to contest the election must have offices in thirteen of the country's (then) twenty-seven provinces and have proof of support by 1 million signatories. Further, parties fail-

61. *Kompas,* 24 November 1998, 11.

ing to gain at least 10 percent of the seats in the House would ineligible to compete at the next election. These provisions were widely criticized as too restrictive and were soon softened.

A greater controversy centered on the provision that civil servants be permitted to vote, but no longer be permitted to join parties or run in elections. GOLKAR fought this stipulation fiercely. The country's 4.1 million civil servants were thought to be mostly GOLKAR supporters and under Suharto had played a vital supporting role in the party. Now an estimated 10,000 people—including party leader, Akbar Tanjung—would be forced to choose between membership in GOLKAR and the retention of their government positions. Interestingly, Habibie (himself a member of GOLKAR) joined the other parties in opposing GOLKAR on this point. Ultimately a compromise was reached whereby the reference to civil servants was dropped altogether and separate regulations specified that civil servants could only join political parties with the approval their immediate superior and then would have to take a leave of absence with basic pay for up to one year, renewable for five years.[62]

The essence of the bill on the composition of the House of Representatives and the Consultative Assembly was to make the two chambers more democratic. Whereas the House's main role was legislative, the Assembly was empowered to choose the president and vice president, amend the constitution, and issue superior laws. The biggest institutional changes were to the Assembly, which was scaled back from 1,000 to 750 members, with the proportion of directly or indirectly elected members jumping from 43 to 95 percent.[63] Henceforth the body that chose the president was to comprise overwhelmingly people chosen by someone other than the president (mostly, voters), a fundamental change from the system in which Suharto chose the majority of people who elected him. The most intense debate on this bill centered on the issue of military representation in the House. The draft bill proposed that the number of appointed military representatives be reduced from 75 to 55. The military itself

62. King (1999, 13–14).
63. Of this total, 66 percent was directly elected by the public as members of the House, and 29 percent was indirectly elected (primarily by popularly elected provincial legislatures) (King 1999, 7).

had already publicly accepted that its representation in the House should be reduced and, separately, was taking steps of its own to decouple itself from GOLKAR and to discontinue the practice of placing active-duty military officers in civilian posts within the government.[64] Although it began as a low-key issue, once continued military representation was taken up by student demonstrators as a symbol of residual antidemocratic practices, the parties began calling for an ever lower number, finally settling on thirty-eight.

The passage of these three laws brought about far-reaching changes in Indonesia's political architecture.[65] To be sure, it fell short of the more radical aspirations of the student movements, but the changes were dramatic nonetheless. At the most elemental level they paved the way for the country's first largely democratic elections since 1955 and, in turn, for the election of a president by a constitutional process he did not control. But more than this, the institutions of government now related to one another in fundamentally different ways. This became very clear as 1999 progressed, with free elections for the House in June followed by the convening of the Assembly in October. It quickly became apparent that the Assembly was now the fulcrum of national politics. Constitutionally, the Assembly had always held great power, but Suharto had skillfully and legally manipulated it by virtue of other subordinate political laws that empowered him to choose a majority of the Assembly—and thus a majority of the people responsible for reelecting him. But with the parties now independent and the president no longer able to control the regional and sectoral representatives, the Assembly rather than the president suddenly emerged as the critical player in the country's altered political configuration.

The Assembly lost no time in asserting itself. In October it decided that, rather than meeting once every five years to select a president as minimally required by the constitution, it would meet annually. There were two main purposes for this: so that the president could

64. Crouch (1999).
65. These three laws were by no means the only important changes to the country's political framework. In April, legislation was passed separating the police from the military, followed in May by legislation devolving significant power to subnational units of government.

appear before the Assembly and present an annual accountability speech[66] and to enable the Assembly to issue decrees and amend the constitution as it saw fit.

Notwithstanding the furious pace of reform in the short period since Suharto's fall, it was clear that there were still many serious unresolved problems in the country's evolving institutional framework. Some of these were created by the compromises embedded in the changes introduced during the initial burst of reforms. For instance, the new electoral system was impossibly convoluted. There was ongoing debate over the division of legislative powers between the president and the House, with many wanting to strengthen the position of the House further. There was considerable ambiguity about the president's relationship with the Assembly, with a number of players pushing for a cleaner system of direct presidential elections. And there were important unresolved details about both the relationship between national and newly empowered subnational units of government (including the possibility of creating an additional legislative chamber for regional representatives) and the phasing out of direct military representation in the House and the Assembly. In short, there were still many institutional issues of fundamental importance to the governance of the country requiring urgent attention. But little headway was made with them in the October 1999 session. The Assembly appointed internal working groups to deliberate on these and other thorny matters prior to its next annual session. Notwithstanding the considerable efforts of these working groups, when the Assembly met as a whole in August 2000, disagreements among the parties again prevented the Assembly from dealing with most of the big issues. The most notable cleavage here was between those who took a more conservative position on constitutional change and those who were anxious to push ahead. The constitutional conservatives comprised Megawati Sukarnoputri's large PDI-P bloc (to the surprise of many) and the military-police bloc of repre-

66. Indeed, it was the Assembly's formal rejection of Habibie's accountability speech at the October 1999 session that killed, at the eleventh hour, the possibility of his being reappointed president. And the following year, the annual accountability exercise also proved contentious for his successor, Abdurahmin Wahid.

sentatives (to the surprise of none). And with these two blocs alone commanding very nearly the one-third of votes in the Assembly needed to defeat any proposed constitutional amendment, change was always going to be difficult.[67]

If we divide the reform process thus far in Indonesia into two phases—the first from late 1998 to early 1999 under Suharto-era politicians and the second from mid-1999 through 2000 under freely elected politicians—the contrast is striking and surprising. Although not without flaws, very much more was achieved in the first phase than in the second. The October 1999 and August 2000 Assembly sessions produced very little agreement on the pressing institutional questions beyond a notable decision to slow the phasing out of military representation. There was now much less public pressure for progress. Free elections had been successfully completed, producing a legitimately constituted House, Assembly, and presidency. In this environment, public focus on arcane, and uninspiring questions of institutional design faded. And the new crop of politicians had little incentive to overcome the obstacles to forging agreement on the outstanding problems. Indeed, the new institutional framework made achieving much agreement more difficult. Why then was the initial reform phase so productive? Against expectations, a collection of politicians who had come to power under the old regime produced rapid agreement on a fundamental restructuring of the political framework that proved broadly acceptable to all the major players. In the absence of an independent body to handle the process, we might expect a less satisfactory outcome. But there were in fact strong constraints on their behavior—if they were to avoid recriminations for the past and were to have any chance of salvaging a political future for themselves in the newly empowered legislature, they would have to reach a quick agreement that they could all accept and that was credible in the eyes of the broader public. Failure to do so was to

67. "Observers Disappointed with MRR's Annual Session," *Jakarta Post,* 19 August 2000. A report by the National Democratic Institute (NDI 2000) provides a helpful overview of the key issues.

invite further rounds of social instability—the protesters were, quite literally, outside their door—and to further put off the prospect of economic rehabilitation.

The radically centralized nature of Indonesia's political architecture had contributed directly to the country's devastating economic collapse, which in turn, was central to the collapse of the regime itself. The economic destruction of 1997–98 is the most powerful and graphic illustration of the potential perils of a radically centralized political framework. As in the Thai case, there was a powerful sense of Indonesia's reform movement being informed and substantially driven by concerns to overcome the governance problems embedded in the old political architecture. The difference of course was that, unlike in Thailand, the central preoccupation of the reformers in Indonesia was to decentralize power—to strip away from the presidency the institutional controls over other actors that it had accreted. Thus we saw the reemergence of the political parties and the rebirth of the House of Representatives and Consultative Assembly. With a variety of motives, the coalition of enthusiastic and not-so-enthusiastic reformers that emerged in 1998 moved to eliminate autocratic and arbitrary governance by redesigning the country's basic political rules to distribute institutional decision-making power among a number of actors.

Finally, although there is much that remains up in the air in Indonesia at the time of writing, it is already apparent that in their determination to avoid the perils of a political framework that radically concentrates decision-making power, Indonesia's reformers may in fact have "overshot" and produced a system that harks back to the highly fragmented multiparty parliamentary framework of the 1950s and that is the functional equivalent of Thailand's framework of the mid-1990s. In short, the key question for Indonesia is whether it is in fact lurching from an extremely centralized institutional configuration all the way over to a heavily fragmented configuration. With the president dependent on continuous support from a substantially fragmented party system for not only legislative cooperation, but for his or her very survival in office, this is emerging as a serious problem. If Indonesia's current cycle of institutional reengineering stops in this position, the chances of a recentralizing authoritarian backlash before long are high.

INSTITUTIONAL CHANGE AND GOVERNANCE

At an empirical level, the narratives I have assembled provide a window onto the dynamics and directions of the intense struggles over the political frameworks in these four countries. For people interested in Southeast Asia this is of some value because it represents the first systematically comparative account of the battles over political architecture during an era of remarkable change within the region. Plainly, there are still many issues to be explored, but this is at least an initial opening up of a largely uncharted area for comparative analysis. At a broader level, if we draw back from the thickets of empirical detail, the cases speak in intriguing ways to our central concerns about the configuration of political institutions and its effect on governance. To see this, we need to consider the net effect of the struggles over political architecture in each country. What, in short, did these episodes mean for the extent to which decision-making power was dispersed? Let us quickly review each case.

Thailand underwent a wide-ranging exercise in political reengineering that is likely to have consequences on many fronts—not all of them desired or intended. Amid the wider change, the overall trend for changes in the configuration of decision-making power is likely to be strongly in the direction of reducing the established pattern of severe and chronic fragmentation. Several factors point in this direction. The most important, over the long term, is the electoral system because it has such a powerful bearing on the incentives of both voters and candidates. As Allen Hicken has shown, the old system with many multimember districts and plurality voting strongly encouraged candidates to campaign on the basis of their own individual ability to deliver benefits to constituents rather than on the basis of their party's collective reputation because they were often

competing against members of their own party.[68] With the elimina-
tion of multimember districts and the adoption of a new mixed-
member electoral system (combining both single-member districts
seats and party-list seats) the incentives for candidates to campaign
on the basis of their party's reputation are much increased.[69] Reinforcing this effect in a much more immediate way is the introduction of new legal and regulatory bodies (principally, the National
Counter Corruption Commission, the Constitutional Court, and the
Electoral Commission) which have the authority to punish illegal
practices such as vote buying. Combined, these changes are likely to
strengthen political parties considerably, giving members a much
greater incentive to cohere and party leaders a greater ability to en-
force cohesion. In addition to encouraging stronger parties, the new
electoral system is likely to encourage fewer parties. In the absence
of deep regional or social cleavages, an electoral system heavily
weighted toward single-member districts with plurality voting dis-
courages multiple parties, as does a provision that the one hundred
party-list seats allocated proportionally only among those parties
gaining at least 5 percent of the national vote. This threshold is a further deterrent to small parties. Also relevant is the unusual constitutional provision whereby members of parliament chosen to be
cabinet ministers must surrender their parliamentary seats. These
and some other procedural rules greatly discourage party defections
from the government because members of cabinet who walk out no
longer have a seat in the House to return to.

The net effect here is that, over time, Thailand is likely to see fewer
and more cohesive parties in parliament. Fewer parties in parliament
means that fewer parties will be required to form a government because the individual parties will also be larger. In addition to requiring fewer parties, governments are likely to have a heightened
measure of stability because of the severe penalties for defection. The
January 2001 election provided the first window onto party politics
in the new environment.[70] In the time leading up to that election,

68. Hicken (1998).
69. Carey and Shugart (1995).
70. There is no country that is an exact comparison with Thailand to provide insights into how the new electoral system will play out, although South Korea, Japan,

my own expectation was that two to three parties would be required to form a government. This turned out to be on target, although, interestingly, Shinawatra Thaksin almost succeeded in governing on the basis of his own Thai Rak Thai party alone. Thaksin and his government have been the subjects of extensive criticism. But whatever we may think of the coalition's character and policy disposition, it is assuredly in a very much better position to get things done. Bringing the analytic lens of a veto player framework to bear, we can say that Thailand now had two to three veto players rather than the six veto players of earlier times.[71] The veto player framework certainly does not capture the impact of all the relevant changes here, but it does offer a rough indicator of the extent of the changes. And regardless of the particular gauge we use, the central point is clear: under the new framework Thailand is moving in from the institutional extremes—away from severe fragmentation toward a more intermediate position.

In the Philippines, various attempts to modify the country's political architecture by Ramos's team were defeated. As such, the configuration of decision-making power remained essentially unchanged. The Philippines retained a moderately fragmented framework that was associated with a reasonably effective pattern of governance under Ramos. Philippine citizens and commentators were far from reluctant to complain about the way in which they were governed, but in the face of a campaign for institutional change there was a powerful consensus in favor of maintaining the status quo.

Malaysia too was a case in which the institutional status quo was preserved—Malaysia retained its heavily centralized configuration. Although there was certainly widespread concern about arbitrary

---

Mexico, and Russia share some key elements with Thailand. These cases generally bear out the core expectations of institutionalist theory about electoral systems, although there is a significant question about how quickly it will play out. See, for instance Reed (1994) and Moser (2001).

71. Although the Senate has been bolstered in various ways, it still has only the power to delay rather reject or amend legislation. Accordingly, with the partial exception of extremely time-sensitive matters (when even a small delay might be consequential) we can leave it aside.

governance in the wake of the economic crisis, these views did not prevail because of a combination of institutional advantages enjoyed by the incumbent party and, more deeply, the existence of cross-cutting ethnic preferences.

With Indonesia we again come to a case of major change. The scale and scope of change was even more sweeping here than in Thailand. If we focus on those elements of change pertaining to the configuration of national decision-making power, it is plain that Indonesia moves in from the extreme of a highly centralized framework. But the specifics of the extent to which it does so are important. Among the many important institutional changes in Indonesia since the fall of Suharto, the most notable for our purposes are the removal of presidential controls on the political parties; the disentangling of state officials (both civilian and military) from direct involvement in political parties and electoral competition; the decision to maintain a proportional representation electoral system; and the removal of the president's power to select those who subsequently selected the president, a result of both the freeing up of the political parties and the selection of regional and functional representatives to the People's Assembly by actors other than the president.

The overall effect of these changes was to boost the power of both the House of Representatives and the People's Assembly (which, recall, comprises the membership of the House plus some regional and sectoral representatives) relative to the presidency. But because of unusual features in the Indonesian framework, they did so in complex ways. The freeing up of the parties meant that the House quickly became a central player for the purposes of legislation; it was no longer a mere agent of the presidency. But the electoral system, reinforced by significant regional and social cleavages, meant that a strongly multiparty system emerged, with five large parties and sixteen smaller ones gaining representation at the 1999 election. Note that compared to the Philippines, the parties were much more likely to behave as coherent blocs in the legislature.[72] A further important

72. Under a PR-list system, candidates have strong incentives to remain loyal to their party and the party leadership can readily punish wayward behavior by placing offenders lower down the list on the party slate at the next election (Carey and Shugart 1995).

twist stems from the unusual position and power of the People's Assembly. With the freeing up of its members, the president was now beholden to the Assembly rather than the other way around—as it had been under Suharto. The agency relationships had been reversed. Under the new rules, winning the presidency required the construction of a majority in the Assembly made up of some combination of parties and military, regional, or functional representatives. Further, because the Assembly had decided, in effect, to review the president's performance on an ongoing basis, the system now had powerful parliamentary characteristics. Quite simply, the president needs to maintain the support of the Assembly to remain in office. And this, of course, has implications for the president's bargaining power with the parties in their more familiar legislative role in the House. Stated bluntly, the president had little ability to twist arms in the House. If we apply a veto player framework, Indonesia now had three to four veto players—the president and, depending on precisely which parties, two to three parties to achieve a majority in the House.[73] As in Thailand, the number of veto players was very sensitive to the number of parties and the extent to which party system consolidated. Making firm statements about Indonesia's political framework at present is of uncertain value because problems inherent in the new framework make it highly likely that it will be subject to further change. Nevertheless, if we draw back to consider the wider picture, it is clear that the overall effect of Indonesia's institutional restructuring has been to shift the country's political framework inward from a position of extreme concentration of decision-making to one of significant fragmentation.

If we now pool the outcomes of our four cases, the outlines of an interesting pattern begin to emerge that ties back to my central argument about the implications of political architecture for governance—the power concentration paradox. Thailand's reforms reduced the average number of parties needed to form a governing coalition and thus reduce the number of veto players from approxi-

73. Because each party determined its position as an independent collective, we treat each as a separate veto player. This is in contrast to the Philippine House, where legislators make their own individual determinations rather than deciding collectively as members of a particular party.

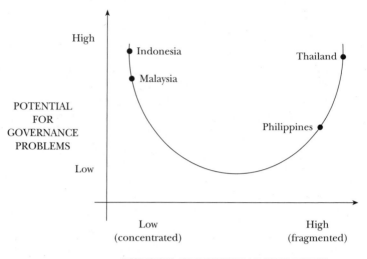

Figure 5.1 Political Configuration Pre-reform

mately six to two to three, and perhaps as low as one to two over time. The Philippines remained unchanged after the defeat of the push for major structural change; Malaysia also remained unchanged. And Indonesia moved from a single veto player framework to one in which there were three to four. Figures 5.1 and 5.2 present this in graphical form, contrasting the before and after political configurations.

Keep in mind that this schematic representation is highly stylized. It offers only a rough guide based on the number of veto players and whether these actors are individuals or collectives. There are many important qualitative dimensions that have not been picked up here; for instance, the effect of various measures that are likely to make coalitions more stable and strengthen the position of the prime minister as the coordinator of the cabinet. But the utility of this technique is that it enables us capture the gross differences among diverse political frameworks in a standardized fashion. With these qualifications in mind, the striking point that emerges is that the two cases with the most extreme institutional configurations were the

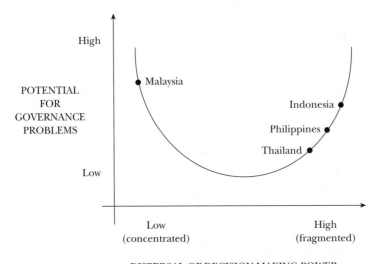

Figure 5.2 Political Configuration Post-reform

ones to undergo substantial institutional redesign and that the effect of this redesign was precisely to pull them in from the margins. That our two outlier cases—Thailand with a severely fragmented framework and Indonesia with a severely centralized framework—both moved in from the extremes is not simply coincidental. In both cases, there was explicit and widespread recognition of the deeply problematic policy syndromes that were associated with their respective institutional configurations—Thai reformers understood all too clearly the deeply dysfunctional implications for governance of their highly fragmented political framework and Indonesian reformers fully appreciated the perils of an institutionally unconstrained leader.

Equally interesting is the fact that in the Philippines a serious institutional reform drive was defeated. For all its imperfections, the Philippine political framework was not an outlier, and, indeed, implicit in the campaign to defend the existing political framework was a recognition that it had not failed and was at some level reasonably functional. Philippine defenders of the institutional status quo may well have regarded it as less than optimal, but they did not consider it grossly dysfunctional and certainly (given their past experiences with dictatorship) they preferred to preserve the existing framework rather than gamble on any of the institutional tinkering that Ramos and his people were pushing. Whether Ramos's proposals would have led the country back to a pattern of dangerously centralized politics is unclear; indeed, it is possible that they may even have been an incremental improvement on the status quo—in effect, moving the country's political architecture a little further inward on our range. But given the options on the table, there was much greater support for retaining the tolerably functional status quo than gambling on the possibility of sliding back toward an excessively powerful presidency.

Due to the enabling effect of a major shock, Thailand's and Indonesia's political frameworks were widely seen to be deeply flawed and these countries were thus candidates for institutional change. The opposite was the case in the Philippines. It was precisely the extreme cases that underwent reform in the wake of the economic upheaval, the distinctive problematic policy syndromes predicted under my model were indeed central concerns for the reform movements, and the institutional solutions they came up with did indeed seem likely to mitigate those particular problems. And in the case furthest from the margins, the defeat of a push to adjust the institutional framework reflected both a fear that major change might move the Philippines back in an unwelcome direction and a recognition that the existing framework was at least tolerably functional.

This is evidence of another sort that offers support for my argument about the implications of political architecture for governance. My primary concern is to make an argument about the effects of institutional configuration, as distinct from an argument about institutional change, but the two are not unrelated. Institutional arrangements that produce systemic governance problems are, sooner or later, likely to be subject to pressures for change, as these four cases show.

In chapter 4 we show how the configuration of decision-making power influences the prevailing pattern of policy making, with cases with severely centralized and severely fragmented configurations giving rise to distinctive and problematic policy syndromes. In this chapter, we have seen evidence of the two cases with the most severely problematic institutional configurations undergoing reform that was explicitly intended to tackle these problems. And in the case with the institutional configuration least likely among our sample to be prone to either extreme policy syndrome, the Philippines, we have seen a determined effort to resist a campaign to alter the political framework precisely because of fears that it might result in a slide back toward a severe centralization of power. To be sure, a small sample of cases such as this can be only suggestive not conclusive, but patterns of this sort demand attention.

I am not proposing a functionalist or evolutionary argument about the dynamics of institutional change whereby better institutional frameworks evolve simply because they are more efficient.[74] I am certainly not suggesting that we can expect some neat and tidy pattern of institutional convergence. All the evidence here about the difficulty of institutional change and the impact of highly contingent factors in shaping outcomes that emerges from the cases themselves warns against any such expectations. And yet to recognize—indeed, to insist on—the importance of contingent factors and the inescapably political nature of the reform process need not prevent us from also recognizing the existence of a wider pattern. As already noted, it seems quite unlikely that it was purely random that the two extreme outliers among our four cases should move in from the margins and that the most intermediate case should resist pressures that were seen as threatening to move it back toward the margins.

This pattern is suggestive of a wider argument that both reinforces and grows out of my central thesis about the U-shaped relationship

---

74. Axelrod captures the essence of evolutionary perspectives on institutional change when he says, "The evolutionary approach is based on a simple principle: whatever is successful is likely to appear more often in the future" (1984, 169). For major exemplars of this approach to institutional change, see Hayek (1979), North and Thomas (1973), Knight (1992), and Knight and Sened (1995). For powerful critiques of functionalist reductionism in evolutionary models of institutional change, see Pierson (2000) and Thelen (1999). For a wider and valuable review of evolutionary models, see Kahler (1999).

between the distribution of institutional decision-making power and governance. Over time, political frameworks that lie toward either extreme of the range are likely to break down or to be torn down, fundamentally because of the deeply problematic governance syndromes they give rise to. Thus, although reformers may have many and varied motives and may be aided at key junctures by unforeseen exogenous shocks, in a sense we can think of them as picking up or perhaps being the bearers of the logic captured in the power concentration paradox. Stated more simply, over time, outlying institutional configurations are likely to be defeated precisely because of the problems to which they are prone. National political architectures that do not work—that are prone to deep and chronic governance problems—are unlikely to endure. And here it is worth remembering that almost all OECD political systems are now located toward the center of our range. Further, it seems unlikely to be just a coincidence that what had been the most striking exceptions have also moved toward the center in recent times—New Zealand (which had a highly centralized framework) has moved in toward the middle, as have Italy and Belgium (both of which had quite fragmented frameworks).[75]

To make this claim is not to imply some linear or teleological trajectory of institutional progress and evolution. The fact that a deeply problematic institutional framework is dislodged is no guarantee that its replacement will be better. Indonesia provides an all-too-distressing illustration of this; it seems to be lurching from one extreme over toward the other. In Indonesia we seem to be witnessing the best efforts of local and international political architects—armed with the best available theory on institutions—being thwarted by the inescapable political imperatives of the parliamentarians. Not only does the new framework look very problematic, it may even invite the prospect of some sort of a recentralizing authoritarian backlash. And in Thailand, incumbent politicians may yet thwart key elements of the constitutional reform. Little noticed in the celebration over the successful adoption of Thailand's new constitution was a clause providing for a very low threshold for further constitutional amend-

75. For details on the changes, see Shugart and Wattenberg (2001a).

ments—they require just a simple majority of the parliament. Although uncontentious at the time, this was part of the price for securing the agreement of conservative members of the drafting assembly and indeed the parliament.[76]

And here we come up against some of the limitations of institutional analysis. The whole thrust of this book has been to argue for the utility of a focus on institutional variables in political analysis. But such an approach also has limits. We see some of this emerge in the consideration of how the Indonesian party system has evolved. We see it even more plainly in the Malaysian case, where the configuration of power is clearly deeply sensitive to social cleavages. Institutional analysis has a great deal to tell us, but it does not tell us everything. And this points us towards a theme I will pick up in the next and final chapter: the limits of institutional analysis.

76. I am grateful to Suchit Bunbongkarn, a member of the CDA steering committee, for this point.

CHAPTER 6

Institutions, Governance, and Beyond

It is time to draw the various threads of this study together. This book is an investigation of a large, elusive, and yet important topic: the consequences of basic differences in national political architecture for key dimensions of governance. What effect does the extent of the dispersal of institutional decision-making power have on a country's overall pattern of policy management? I have attacked this question in three ways.

First, stimulated by inherent theoretical tensions between two big currents of institutional scholarship—commitment-type claims and decisiveness-type claims—I have developed an argument on a deductive basis. I labeled this argument the power concentration paradox. In essence, I have proposed that there is a curvilinear, or U-shaped, relationship between the extent of the dispersal of decision-making power and the propensity for serious governance problems. That is, political frameworks that either severely centralize or severely fragment decision-making power are much more likely to be prone to damaging patterns of policy behavior. These damaging policy syndromes are distinctive and can be inferred from the essential features of a country's political architecture. Institutional configurations that severely centralize power are more prone to problems of policy volatility, whereas configurations that severely fragment power are more prone to problems of policy rigidity. Although these conditions are polar opposites, either can be very costly.

Second, I have introduced an empirical analysis, using Thailand,

the Philippines, Malaysia, and Indonesia as case studies, of an overall pattern of policy behavior in response to a major common challenge, the tremendous economic instability of the 1997–98 Asian
economic crisis. I have introduced a veto player analysis to provide
a standardized gauge for comparing the extent of the dispersal of
institutionalized decision-making authority across the very diverse
political architectures of these four cases. These ranged from the
highly fragmented political configuration in Thailand to the moderately fragmented framework in the Philippines to the highly centralized framework in Malaysia and to the even more highly centralized
framework in Indonesia. Armed with these institutional profiles,
we have explored the responses of governments in each country to
the unfolding economic crisis, tracing the policy outcomes back
to national political architectures. The findings of these various analytic narratives are quite striking. The broad patterns of policy management in each case corresponded to a remarkable extent with the
original theoretical intuition: Thailand exhibited a pattern of debilitating policy rigidity, Malaysia and Indonesia exhibited severe
problems of policy volatility, and the Philippines exhibited neither
extreme syndrome but a satisfactory if messy intermediate pattern.

Third, I have introduced an empirical analysis from a different
angle, this time connecting political architecture and institutional
reform. I have explored pressures for and processes of institutional
change in the four countries, largely in the wake of the seismic shock
of the regional economic crisis. Which institutional configurations
from among our sample have been subject to change, and why?
Equally, which configurations have emerged unchanged, and why?
Again the results are striking. Our two extreme, or outlier, cases—
Thailand and Indonesia—both underwent processes of fundamental institutional redesign. In each case, the powerful underlying im-
pulse was to overcome the governance problems embedded in the
old political architecture and the effect of the institutional redesign
was to pull the configuration of decision-making authority in from
their previous outlier positions. In Malaysia, incipient pressures in
this direction were outweighed by cross-cutting concerns about preserving ethnic interests. In the Philippines, a push for institutional
reform was defeated precisely because of fears it would result in the

country's political configuration being pulled back in the direction of a dangerous centralization of decision-making power. The overall picture that emerges from this set of analytic narratives provides support of a quite different sort for my theory about the implications of institutions for governance. Growing out of direct experience, there was recognition by reformers of the practical governance problems of institutional frameworks that severely fragment or severely concentrate decision-making authority. Although there were, assuredly, many considerations in play in each case, we can see this logic as a powerful element in struggles over institutional redesign.

A U-shaped relationship between institutional configuration and governance gives us the theoretical link with which to reconcile the underlying tension in the literature between commitment-type arguments and decisiveness-type arguments. Further, it allows us to extend the literature in interesting ways by connecting institutions to policy in a generalizable fashion. To a remarkable extent, commitments-type arguments and decisiveness-type arguments have been made in isolation of one another, almost passing as ships in the night. Positing a continuous curvilinear relationship allows us to overcome this discontinuity. The fundamental insight of the commitments literature is that political configurations that concentrate power carry major risks of arbitrary and capricious governance. Dispersing decision-making power reduces the likelihood of these problems. Expressed in the more precise terms of a veto player framework, moving from one individual veto player to one collective veto player and adding additional veto players has this effect. But only up to a point —some unspecified point of inflexion (or, more realistically, zone of inflexion)—after which the further dispersal of decision-making power begins to again increase the risk of governance problems, the problems of delay and paralysis with which the decisiveness literature deals. The risk of either of these deeply problematic patterns of governance rises as we move toward either end of the range of possible institutional configurations, thus giving us a U-shaped relationship. This is the heart of the power concentration paradox.

My purpose here is not to suggest that any specific institutional configuration will provide optimal outcomes. I have certainly argued, in broad terms, that institutional configurations located toward the middle of the range are, other things equal, to be preferred because they are less prone to either of the deeply problematic governance syndromes outlined. But there are important caveats here. I definitely do not mean to imply that any particular country has the ideal national political architecture. Such a claim, even if meaningful, is beyond the scope of this study; it would require a level of specificity that I have self-consciously eschewed. My focus has been the gross institutional characteristics of national political architecture; once we drop to a more fine-grained focus it quickly becomes apparent that there is very considerable microinstitutional variation within just the intermediate portion of the range. Recall that in terms of the analytical metric of the veto player framework, national political architectures with two to three veto players are considered the middle of the range. But note that this segment of the range alone encompasses almost all the political systems of the advanced industrial world. To even begin to form a serious preference for a particular national political architecture over others we would need to come to grips with the significance of the more microinstitutional features that differentiate them.

But that is not my concern; my concern is with the broader picture, operating at a higher level of aggregation, focusing on gross institutional features and their implications for governance. And, in this, my attention has been directed primarily toward the two ends of the range rather than the middle—in other words with those sections of the range most likely to be inhabited by developing countries.

The arguments developed here have significant implications for both the world of praxis and the world of scholarship. In practical terms, this study speaks to consumers of policy in developing countries—be they citizens, investors, foreign governments, or international agencies. It draws attention to the systematic implications of macropolitical institutions for governance, highlighting specific problematic syndromes that are characteristic of political architectures at either end of the range. In this sense, instead of a message of "here lies perfection," this study takes more the form "in either of these directions lie dragons." A country with a political framework that severely fragments decision-making power—such as Thailand's (before its recent reforms) or, increasingly, Indonesia's (since its re-forms)—faces extraordinary difficulties in adjusting policy settings in a timely and effective manner. Understanding this allows citizens, investors, and would-be international collaborators to better assess governance risks. And knowing precisely where the choke points in the system are holds out some hope of perhaps crafting reform pro-posals in a way that makes their passage less difficult. Conversely, al-though a highly centralized framework—such as Indonesia's (under Suharto) or Malaysia's (still)—certainly allows rapid and flexible pol-icy adjustment, anyone looking to secure commitments from such governments must be alert to the dramatically increased risk that pol-icy makers will renege on their promises and reverse policy course outright. Policy commitments are much harder to reverse when the agreement of multiple independent actors is required. In the ab-sence of such institutional checks, it may be possible to devise ad hoc institutional devices or arrangements that trigger serious costs in the event of policy reversal. Failing this, however, high governance risks are inescapable. And, in between, countries such as the Philippines and (now) Thailand, whose political architectures lie in from the two extremes, toward the center of the range, are, on average, much more amenable to stable policy adjustment and international coop-eration. The institutional barriers to achieving political consensus are not impossibly high, and those preventing a reversal of commit-ments are meaningful.

These are broad tendencies. Political reality is, of course, not so neat and tidy that these propositions hold unbreakably in all cir-cumstances. A variety of other factors may exert an intervening influ-ence, ranging from the effect of individual political leadership skills to circumstantial contingencies. A dramatic contemporary illustra-tion of this is the operation of U.S. government in the immediate af-termath of the September 11 terrorist attacks. In the weeks after the attack we saw an extraordinary level of cross-party and cross-institu-tional policy cooperation, enabling what was (by U.S. standards) ex-tremely rapid policy adjustment. A dramatic shock can exert a powerful influence on the business of government. And yet we also know that under normal circumstances the U.S. political framework is very much slower to make and unmake legislative commitments.

The power concentration paradox alerts us to broad tendencies, but these are tendencies that consumers of policy in developing countries—from the IMF down—would do well to consider.

Turning from the world of policy and praxis to the realm of scholarly research, this study seeks to push the literature in a number of ways. At the most general level, it makes a case for much more sustained attention to institutionally focused research in developing countries. I have already noted that developing countries are more likely to be affected by the twin perils of the power concentration paradox because they are more likely to have national political architectures that severely concentrate or fragment decision-making power. Further, and contrary to the conventional wisdom, I suggest that the configuration of national political architecture is in fact particularly consequential for developing countries. The way in which Leviathan makes up its mind matters in all polities, but it is especially consequential in developing countries because the state has so much greater potential to help or harm. On the demand side of policy, the list of major problems crying out for attention is truly daunting; on the supply side, with the surrounding public and private institutional landscape being much more sparse, the state looms so much larger in both economic and political life. Thus, although the bulk of institutional scholarship has overwhelmingly focused on advanced industrial polities, the challenge for the future is to push more aggressively and creatively into the realm of developing-country politics.

Beyond this general argument for more analytic attention to developing-country polities, my power concentration paradox thesis points to a quite specific agenda for future research in this area. Although my four countries have lent themselves handily to the needs of comparative research, it is clear that this study is more an exercise in theory building than theory testing. My case-based qualitative analysis has been driven by both my fascination with these countries and the desire to be able to unpack policy processes. The advantage of this approach is that it permits me to illustrate convincingly likely causal connections, but its limitation is that it does not permit any wider verification that might be offered by large-n statistical analysis. My contribution is to make a plausible and generalizable theoretical case. But there is a much wider research agenda here begging for the attention of others with quantitative skills and tastes. We already have large-n statistical work supporting the idea that additional veto players reduce policy volatility problems.[1] But because this research grows out of commitments-type theorizing, it has (understandably) not tested for the possibility that there can be too much of a good thing—that veto players can be oversupplied and that beyond some zone of inflexion we encounter increasingly serious problems of policy rigidity. My work points to the need for statistical investigation in both directions.

In addition to statistical testing of the arguments, there is also much scope for theoretical refinement. One direction for this is exploring the possibility of sector-specific variation in the force of the power concentration paradox. Significant value could be added by comparing the impact of institutional configuration across different sorts of policy sectors. For instance, collective goods–type policies such as monetary policy or international security alliances as opposed to more divisible private goods–type policies such as trade policy or public works expenditure. Another line of investigation centers on analytic technology. I have employed a veto player framework as my primary analytic tool for calibrating the extent of the dispersal of institutional decision-making authority. Although this has many advantages, inevitably it highlights certain features and obscures others. One issue in particular that may yield rewards for further investigation is the possible significance of differences between individual and collective veto players: How much difference does it make if the proximate decision maker is a single person rather than a collective of people that must decide as a unit? Another interesting issue is the possible significance of differences between bargaining among actors located in the same institutional arena (e.g., coalition partners in a parliament) and actors that are institutionally separated (e.g., bicameralism and presidentialism).[2]

1. The key work here is Witold Henisz (2000a), and discussions with Henisz have been helpful in the development of my own thinking. For other work in this vein, see the literature cited in chapter 2.

2. Crepaz (1998; Birchfield and Crepaz 1998) has begun the investigation of this question.

More broadly, although a veto player framework is the best available analytic technology for a comparative study of this sort, there is certainly room for refinement. Once we step away from political architectures that are replicas or close approximations of the most well-known North American and European models, careful empirical specification quickly becomes crucial. The application to some cases is not straightforward, particularly on the issue of whether decisions are made collectively or not. This is especially so with semidemocratic and nondemocratic regimes, in which appearances can sometimes be quite deceiving. (This is a particularly important consideration for statistical analysis.) Consider cases such as China and Singapore, both of which have powerful Leninist party structures. On what basis are decisions made and what is the range of actors that has the inalienable institutional authority to veto policy change? In these and a surprising number of other cases, the specification of the basis of decision making is not immediately apparent and is likely to require careful empirical investigation. I have made some modest suggestions in this study regarding a strictly institutionalist application of a veto player framework, but no doubt we can look forward to further refinement in this method of analysis as its application is extended geographically.

Interwoven through the development of the theoretical claims of this study have been empirical narratives of an extraordinary period in the political and economic histories of Thailand, the Philippines, Malaysia, and Indonesia. An institutional window onto the Southeast Asian world has afforded fresh and powerful perspectives on the great dramas of the era—enormous economic upheaval and the ongoing struggle over the organization of political life. We have seen how political architecture—a variable largely ignored in the scholarly literature on this part of the world—exerted a powerful influence on the handling of the economic crisis of 1997–98. And we have seen the way in which these considerations fed back into the battles over political reform. The drama of the economic crisis was not just about the strengths and weaknesses of individual political leaders and political factions or specific policy settings or even sets of local and foreign economic interests connected in various ways to governments. No doubt, all of these factors played a role. But what has been missing from the country-specific accounts of this episode —and, indeed, of most discussions about politics more generally in Southeast Asia—is the silent but persistent effect of institutional arrangements on policy outcomes. And in this, there is a peculiar disconnect between the literature and the drama of real-life politics on the ground in these countries; it is precisely the rules of the political game that have been at the center of so much of the heaving and pulling in the late twentieth and early twenty-first centuries. These struggles are unlikely to end any time soon, as long-term processes of political change and consolidation continue to be played out. This speaks powerfully to the need for institutional variables to be brought into the mainstream of scholarly thinking about Southeast Asian politics in a serious way.

In this account, some students of Southeast Asian politics may miss the rich texture and empirical detail that is characteristic of the best single-country studies. Others may miss the substance of conflicting interests and ideas. In exchange, I offer the analytic gains that come both from trading single-country depth for comparative breadth and the new insights afforded by an institutionalist window on political life. My focus has been on the implications of national political architecture for governance, but there is a much wider institutionalist research agenda here for political scientists with a particular interest in this part of the world. I very much hope that this book helps in some measure to open this research frontier further in Southeast Asia. There is much to be done. Consider, for a moment, the numerous questions pertaining to the design of institutional powers among national and subnational political units, the questions pertaining to the position of the judiciary and the possibility of independent legal systems, or, at a more microlevel, the enormous importance of the details of electoral rules for the nature of party systems. Encouragingly, there are signs of an emerging cohort of younger scholars that is likely to push much further in exploring the effects of various formal political institutions on the basis of Southeast Asian countries.[3]

3. For example, Allen Hicken (at UCSD) is working on the effects of the party system on the provision of public goods–type policies using case studies from Thailand

I have maintained an unremitting analytical focus on political institutions throughout this study. This has been a deliberate research strategy; I have favored tight advocacy over broad illumination. In order to make my case about political architecture, institutions were brought to the foreground so that we might see more clearly their effects. Inevitably, there is an element of artificiality inherent in such an approach—with other factors having received less attention as a result. But this issue ultimately turns on what I am trying to achieve in this book. At the outset, I narrowly justify my approach by noting that, in a macro sense, the comparability of the profiles of these four countries along other major dimensions facilitated the focus on institutions. More fundamentally, however, my basic objectives for this book have dictated the research strategy. One approach for political scientists is to strive to capture the full complexity of politics—to identify all the factors at play and how they interact with one another to produce a certain outcome at a particular place and time. Another is to simplify and to strive for analytic parsimony—to isolate the effect of some factor, or set of factors, in a way that might lend itself to some degree of generalization and application to other situations. Each approach has its merits and advocates. For this study, my approach has been much more in the direction of the latter than the former. My primary goal has been to think about the effects of institutions, rather than to explain particular events.

Yet, plainly, institutional perspectives on politics have their limits. Institutions do not cause outcomes on their own: they set the framework within which contending interests do battle. Interests, and the ideas that lie behind them, are the fundamental drivers in political life. Malaysia's experiences in the wake of the economic crisis provide a useful reminder of the limits of institutional analysis. Although

---

and the Philippines; Yuko Kasuyo (at UCSD) is exploring causal linkages between the weakness of the Philippine party system and the strength of the presidency; Erik Kuhonta (at Princeton University) is exploring the effects of party system differences across the Philippines, Thailand, and Malaysia; Bryan Ritchie (at Emory University) is examining the interactive effects of coalition structures and political institutions on the provision of technical education in Thailand, Malaysia, Singapore, and Indonesia; and Shanker Satyanath (at Columbia University) is working on the institutional foundations of moral hazards in central banking, drawing in part on data from Indonesia, Thailand, Malaysia, and the Philippines.

the highly arbitrary and even capricious behavior of the Malaysian government through 1997–98 was a powerful illustration to Malaysians of the dangers inherent in a political architecture that so centralized decision-making power, cross-cutting interests and ideas about ethnic stability outweighed other governance concerns. The institutional analysis I have been working with can tell us little about this.

A second useful illustration on the limits of institutional analysis comes from the Philippines. I have argued that, compared to Thailand, the less-fragmented configuration of decision-making authority in the Philippines had an important bearing on the ability of Ramos to provide a reasonably coherent and timely response to the regional economic instability. But as the bumbling, tardy, and short-lived administration of Ramos's successor, Joseph Estrada, reminds us, although political architecture sets the parameters of what is possible, it does not tell us what will happen. Institutions tell us nothing about the preferences and aptitudes that individual politicians bring to office.

Like any perspective on politics, institutional analysis has its limits. It is important—especially for those working within an institutional framework—to be conscious of this. But at this stage there is still much to be done before we come up against these limits, both in adding to the toolkit of political science theory and in understanding what is happening in particular regions, such as Southeast Asia. I close with a final Southeast Asian illustration of just how much institutional approaches can add to the study and praxis of politics in developing countries: the deeply troubled situation in Indonesia at the beginning of the twenty-first century. Although Indonesia plainly faces multiple large-scale problems as it struggles to escape the legacy of authoritarianism, rebuild its economy, and heal its social wounds, perhaps the most basic are the enormous obstacles to effective policy leadership embedded in its current political architecture. Regardless of the merits of any individual leader, coalition of parties, pattern of social cleavage, or alignment of international forces, as currently configured, the country's political architecture virtually precludes the possibility of effective governance. There are many variants on this problem in the developing world; political science can make a much greater contribution to thinking about them and tackling them.

References

Abad, Florencio. 1997. "Should the Philippines Turn Parliamentary: The Challenge of Democratic Consolidation and Institutional Reform." In *Shift*, edited by Solimon Santos, Florencio Abad, Joel Rocamora, and Chay Florentino-Hofilena, 48–89. Ateneo Center for Social Policy and Public Affairs, Quezon City.

Acharya, Amitav. 2001. *Constructing a Security Community in Southeast Asia: ASEAN and the Problem of Regional Order.* Routledge, London.

Alburo, Florian. 1998. "The Asian Financial Crisis and Policy Responses in the Philippines." *Philippine Review of Economics and Business* 35(1): 62–86.

Alt, James, and Robert Lowry. 1994. "Divided Government, Fiscal Institutions, and Budget Deficits—Evidence from the States." *American Political Science Review* 88: 811–28.

Ammar, Siamwalla. 1997. *Why Are We in This Mess?* J. Douglas Gibson Lecture, School of Policy Studies, Queen's University, Ontario.

Amsden, Alice. 1990. *Asia's Next Giant: South Korea and Late Industrialization.* Oxford University Press, New York.

Anderson, Benedict. 1990. *Language and Power: Exploring Political Cultures in Indonesia.* Cornell University Press, Ithaca.

Anek, Laothamatas. 1992. *Business Associations and the New Political Economy of Thailand.* Westview, Boulder.

——. 1996. "A Tale of Two Democracies: Conflicting Perceptions of Elections and Democracy in Thailand." In *The Politics of Elections in Southeast Asia,* edited by Robert Taylor, 201–23. Cambridge University Press, New York.

Anusorn, Limmanee. 1998. "Thailand." In *Political Party Systems and Democratic Development in East and Southeast Asia,* edited by Wolfgang Sachsenroder and Ulrike Frings, Vol. 1, 403–48. Ashgate, Aldershot.

Ashford, Douglas. 1981. *Policy and Politics in Britain: The Limits of Consensus.* Temple University Press, Philadelphia.

Athukorala, Prema-chandra. 1998. "Malaysia." In *East Asia in Crisis: From Being a Miracle to Needing One?* edited by Ross McLeod and Ross Garnaut, 85–104. Routledge, London.

Auerswald, David. 1999. "Domestic Institutions and Military Conflicts." *International Organization* 53(3): 469–504.

Avant, Deborah. 1994. *Political Institutions and Military Change: Lessons from Peripheral Wars.* Cornell University Press, Ithaca.

Axelrod, Robert. 1984. *The Evolution of Cooperation.* Basic Books, New York.

Bartlett, Beatrice. 1991. *Monarchs and Ministers: The Grand Council in Mid-Ch'ing China.* University of California Press, Berkeley.

Bates, Robert, Avner Greif, Margaret Levi, Jean-Laurent Rosenthal, and Barry Weingast. 1998. "Introduction." In *Analytic Narratives,* edited by Robert Bates, Avner Greif, Margaret Levi, Jean-Laurent Rosenthal, and Barry Weingast, 3–22. Princeton University Press, Princeton.

Bergara, Mario, Witold Henisz, and Pablo Spiller. 1998. "Political Institutions and Electric Utility Investment." *California Management Review* 40(2): 18–35.

Bernholz, Peter. 1993. "Constitutions as Governance Structures: The Political Foundations of Secure Markets—Comment." *Journal of Institutional and Theoretical Economics* 149(1): 312–20.

Bhanupong, Nidhiprabha. 1998. "Economic Crises and the Debt-Inflation Episode in Thailand." *ASEAN Economic Bulletin* 15(3): 309–18.

Birchfield, Vicki, and Markus Crepaz. 1998. "The Impact of Constitutional Structures and Collective and Competitive Veto Points on Income Inequality in Industrialized Democracies." *European Journal of Political Research* 34(2): 175–200.

Bolongaita, Emil. 1995. "Presidential versus Parliamentary Democracy." *Philippine Studies* 43(1): 105–23.

Borner, Silvio, Aymo Brunetti, and Beatrice Weder. 1995. *Political Credibility and Economic Development.* St. Martin's Press, New York.

Bowie, Alasadair. 1991. *Crossing the Industrial Divide: State, Society, and the Politics of Economic Transformation in Malaysia.* Columbia University Press, New York.

Brennan, Geoffrey, and James Buchanan. 1985. *The Reason of Rules: Constitutional Political Economy.* Cambridge University Press, New York.

Brooks, Risa. 1999. "Institutions Inside Out: The Domestic Origins and International Effects of Political-Military Relations." Ph.D. diss., Department of Political Science, University of California, San Diego.

Burki, Shahid Javed, and Guillermo Perry. 1998. *Beyond the Washington Consensus: Institutions Matter.* World Bank, Washington, D.C.

Cain, Bruce, John Ferejohn, and Morris Fiorina. 1987. *The Personal Vote: Constituency Service and Electoral Independence.* Cambridge University Press, New York.

Calvo, Guillermo. 1978. "On the Time Consistency of Optimal Policy in a Monetary Economy." *Econometrica* 46: 1411–28.

Campos, J. Edgardo, ed. 2001. *Corruption: The Boom and Bust of East Asia.* Ateneo University Press, Manila.

Carey, John, and Matthew Shugart. 1995. "Incentives to Cultivate a Personal Vote: A Rank Ordering of Electoral Formulas." *Electoral Studies* 14(4): 417–39.

———, eds. 1998. *Executive Decree Authority.* Cambridge University Press, New York.

Case, William. 1996. "UMNO Paramountcy: A Report on Single Party Dominance in Malaysia." *Party Politics* 2(1): 115–27.

———. 2001. "Malaysia's General Election in 1999: A Consolidated and High-Quality Semi-Democracy." *Asian Studies Review* 25(1): 35–55.

Chang, Ha-Joon. 2000. "The Hazard of Moral Hazard: Untangling the Asian Crisis." *World Development* 28(4): 775–88.

Christensen, Scott, David Dollar, Amar Siamwalla, and Pakoin Vichyanond. 1993. *Thailand: The Institutional Underpinnings of Growth.* World Bank, Washington, D.C.

Clague, Christopher, ed. 1997. *Institutions and Economic Development: Growth and Governance in Less-Developed and Post-Socialist Countries.* Johns Hopkins University Press, Baltimore.

Clark, David. 1999. "The Many Meanings of the Rule of Law." In *Law, Capitalism and Power in Asia: The Rule of Law and Legal Institutions,* edited by Kanishka Jayasuriya, 28–44. Routledge, London.

Collier, Ruth, and David Collier. 1991. *Shaping the Political Arena: Critical Junctures, the Labor Movement, and Regime Dynamics in Latin America.* Princeton University Press, Princeton.

Connors, Michael K. 1999. "Political Reform and the State in Thailand." *Journal of Contemporary Asia* 29(2): 202–26.

Coronel, Sheila, ed. 1998. *Pork and Other Perks: Corruption and Governance in the Philippines.* Philippines Center for Investigative Journalism, Quezon City.

Cowhey, Peter. 1993. "Domestic Institutions and the Credibility of International Commitments: Japan and the United States." *International Organization* 47(2): 299–326.

Cox, Gary. 1997. *Making Votes Count: Strategic Coordination in the World's Electoral Systems.* Cambridge University Press, New York.

Cox, Gary, and Matthew McCubbins. 2001. "The Institutional Determinants of Policy Outcomes." In *Presidents, Parliaments, and Policy,* edited by Stephan Haggard and Matthew McCubbins, 21–63. Cambridge University Press, New York.

Crepaz, Markus. 1998. "Inclusion versus Exclusion: Political Institutions and Welfare Expenditures." *Comparative Politics* 31(1): 61–80.

Crouch, Harold. 1996. *Government and Society in Malaysia.* Cornell University Press, Ithaca.

———. 1999. "Wiranto and Habibie: Military-Civilian Relations since May 1998."

In *Reformasi: Crisis and Change in Indonesia,* edited by Arief Budiman, Barbara Hatley, and Damien Kingsbury, 127–48. Monash Asia Institute, Monash University, Clayton.

——. 2000. "Indonesia: Democratization and the Threat of Disintegration." In *Southeast Asian Affairs 1999.* Institute of Southeast Asian Studies, Singapore.

Crozier, Michel, Samuel Huntington, and Joji Watanuki. 1975. *The Crisis of Democracy: Report on the Governability of Democracies to the Trilateral Commission.* New York University Press, New York.

de Dios, Emmanuel. 1999. "Executive-Legislative Relations in the Philippines: Continuity and Change." In *Institutions and Economic Change in Southeast Asia: The Context of Development from the 1960s to the 1990s,* edited by Colin Barlow, 132–49. Edward Elgar, Cheltenham.

de Dios, Emmanuel, Benjamin Diokno, Raul Fabella, Felipe Medalla, and Solita Monsod. 1997. "Exchange Rate Policy: Recent Failures and Future Tasks." *Public Policy* 1(1): 15–41.

de Dios, Emmanuel, and Hadi Salehi Esfahani. 2001. "Government and Investment in the Philippines." In *Corruption: The Boom and Bust of East Asia,* edited by J. Edgardo Campos, Ateneo University Press, Manila.

Delhaise, Philippe. 1998. *Asia in Crisis: The Implosion of the Banking and Finance Systems.* John Wiley, Singapore.

Democracy Development Committee. 1995. *A Proposed Framework for Political Reform in Thailand* [in Thai]. Office for Research Support and the Democracy Development Committee, Bangkok.

Deyo, Frederic. 1987. *The Political Economy of the New Asian Industrialism.* Cornell University Press, Ithaca.

Doner, Richard. 1991. *Driving a Bargain: Automotive Industrialization and Japanese Firms in Southeast Asia.* University of California Press, Berkeley.

——. 1992. "The Limits of State Strength: Toward an Institutionalist View of Economic Development." *World Politics* 44(3): 398–431.

Doner, Richard, and Anek Laothamatas. 1994. "Thailand: Economic and Political Gradualism." In *Voting for Reform: Democracy, Political Liberalization, and Economic Adjustment,* edited by Stephan Haggard and Steven Webb, 411–52. Oxford University Press, New York.

Doner, Richard, and Ansil Ramsay. 1999. "Thailand: From Economic Miracle to Economic Crisis." In *Asian Contagion: The Causes and Consequences of a Financial Crisis,* edited by Karl Jackson, 171–205. Westview, Boulder.

Duverger, Maurice. 1954. *Political Parties: Their Organization and Activity in the Modern State.* John Wiley, New York.

Elster, Jon. 1979. *Ulysses and the Sirens: Studies in Rationality and Irrationality.* Cambridge University Press, London.

Emmerson, Donald. 1995. "Singapore and the 'Asian Values' Debate." *Journal of Democracy* 6(4): 95–105.

Ertman, Thomas. 1997. *Birth of the Leviathan: Building States and Regimes in Medieval and Early Modern Europe.* Cambridge University Press, New York.

Evans, Peter, Dietrich Rueschemeyer, and Theda Skocpol, eds. 1985. *Bringing the State Back In*. Cambridge University Press, New York.

Fane, George, and Ross McLeod. 1999. "Lessons for Monetary and Banking Policies from the 1997–98 Crises in Indonesia and Thailand." Paper presented to the American Economic Association, 3–5 January, New York.

Fearon, James. 1994. "Domestic Political Audiences and the Escalation of International Disputes." *American Political Science Review* 88(3): 577–92.

Felker, Greg. 1999. "Malaysia in 1998: A Cornered Tiger Bares Its Claws." *Asian Survey* 39(1): 43–54.

Florentino-Hofilena, Chay. 1997. "Tracking the Charter Amendment Debates (1995—Mid-March 1997)." In *Shift*, edited by Soliman Santos, Florencia Asad, Joel Rocamora, and Chay Florentino-Hofilena, 134–70. Ateneo Center for Social Policy and Public Affairs, Quezon City.

Funston, John. 1999. "Malaysia: A Fateful September." In *Southeast Asian Affairs 1999*, 165–84. Institute of Southeast Asian Studies, Singapore.

———. 2000. "Malaysia's Tenth Elections: Status Quo, Reformasi or Islamization?" *Contemporary Southeast Asia* 22(1): 23–59.

Geddes, Barbara. 1994. *Politician's Dilemmas: Building State Capacity in Latin America*. University of California Press, Berkeley.

———. 1995. "A Comparative Perspective on the Leninist Legacy in Eastern Europe." *Comparative Political Studies* 28(2): 239–75.

Gomez, Edmund Terence. 1998. "Malaysia." In *Political Party Systems and Democratic Development in East and Southeast Asia*, edited by Wolfgang Sachsenroder and Ulrike Frings, Vol. 1, 226–88. Ashgate, Aldershot.

Gomez, Edmund Terrence, and Jomo K. S. 1997. *Malaysia's Political Economy: Politics, Patronage, and Profits*. Cambridge University Press, Cambridge, UK.

Gourevitch, Peter. 1986. *Politics in Hard Times: Comparative Responses to International Economic Crises*. Cornell University Press, Ithaca.

Grenville, Stephen. 1999. "Capital Flows and Crises." *Asian-Pacific Economic Literature* 13(12): 1–15.

Grilli, Vittorio, Donato Masciandaro, and Guido Tabellini. 1991. "Political and Monetary Institutions and Public Financial Policies in the Industrial Countries." *Economic Policy* 6(2): 342–91.

Grindle, Merilee. 2000. *Audacious Reforms: Institutional Invention and Democracy in Latin America*. Johns Hopkins University Press, Baltimore.

Hadiz, Vedi. 1999. "Contesting Political Change after Suharto." In *Reformasi: Crisis and Change in Indonesia*, edited by Arief Budiman, Barbara Hatley, and Damien Kingsbury, 105–26. Monash Asia Institute, Monash University, Clayton.

Haggard, Stephan. 1990. *Pathways from the Periphery: The Politics of Growth in the Newly Industrializing Countries*. Cornell University Press, Ithaca.

———. 2000. *The Political Economy of the Asian Financial Crisis*. Institute for International Economics, Washington, D.C.

Haggard, Stephan, and Robert Kaufman, eds. 1992. *The Politics of Economic Adjustment*. Princeton University Press, Princeton.

——. 1995. *The Political Economy of Democratic Transitions.* Princeton University Press, Princeton.

Haggard, Stephan, and Linda Low. 1999. "The Political Economy of Malaysian Capital Controls." Graduate School of International Relations and Pacific Studies, University of California, San Diego, unpublished manuscript.

Haggard, Stephan, and Andrew MacIntyre. 2001. "The Politics of Moral Hazard: The Origins of the Financial Crisis in Indonesia, Korea, and Thailand." In *Tigers in Distress: The Political Economy of the East Asian Crisis and Its Aftermath,* edited by Arvid Lukauskas and Francisco Rivera-Batiz, 85–109. Edward Elgar, London.

Haggard, Stephan, and Matthew McCubbins, eds. 2001. *Presidents, Parliaments, and Policy.* Cambridge University Press, New York.

Haggard, Stephan, and Steven Webb, eds. 1994. *Voting for Reform: Democracy, Political Liberalisation, and Economic Adjustment.* Oxford University Press, New York.

Hamilton-Hart, Natasha. 2000. "Indonesia: Reforming the Institutions of Financial Governance." In *The Asian Financial Crisis and the Architecture of Global Finance,* edited by Gregory Noble and John Ravenhill, 108–31. Cambridge University Press, Melbourne.

Hayek, Frederich von. 1979. *Law, Legislation, and Liberty: The Political Order of a Free People.* University of Chicago Press, Chicago.

Henisz, Witold. 2000a. "The Institutional Environment for Economic Growth." *Economics and Politics* 12(1): 1–31.

——. 2000b. "The Institutional Environment for Multinational Investment." *Journal of Law, Economics, and Organization* 16(2): 334–64.

Hewison, Kevin, ed. 1997. *Political Change in Thailand: Democracy and Paricipation.* London: Routledge.

——. 2000. "Thailand's Capitalism before and after the Economic Crisis." In *Politics and Markets in the Wake of the Asian Crisis,* edited by Richard Robison, Mark Beeson, Kanishka Jayasuriya, and Hyuk-Rae Kim, 192–211. Routledge, London.

Hicken, Allen. 1998. "From Patronage to Policy: Political Institutions and Policy Making in Thailand." Paper presented at the Midwest Political Science Association Annual Meeting, 23–25 April, Chicago.

——. 1999. "Political Parties and Linkage: Strategic Coordination in Thailand." Paper presented at the annual meeting of the American Political Science Association, 2–5 September, Atlanta.

——. 2001. "Parties, Policy, and Patronage: Governance and Growth in Thailand." In *Corruption: The Boom and Bust of East Asia,* edited by J. Edgardo Campos, Ateneo University Press, Manila.

——. 2002. "Party Systems, Political Institutions, and Policy: Policymaking in Developing Democracies." Ph.D. diss., Graduate School of International Relations and Pacific Studies, University of California, San Diego.

Hill, Hal. 1999. *The Indonesian Economy in Crisis: Causes, Consequences, and Lessons.* Institute of Southeast Asian Studies, Singapore.

Huber, Evelyn, Charles Ragin, and John Stephens. 1993. "Social Democracy, Christian Democracy, and the Welfare State." *American Sociological Review* 9(3): 711–49.

Huntington, Samuel. 1968. *Political Order in Changing Societies.* New Haven, Yale University Press.

Hutchcroft, Paul. 1998. *Booty Capitalism: The Politics of Banking in the Philippines.* Cornell University Press, Ithaca.

——. 1999. "Neither Dynamo Nor Domino? Reform and Crisis in the Philippine Political Economy." In *The Politics of the Asian Economic Crisis,* edited by T. J. Pempel, 163–83. Cornell University Press, Ithaca.

Ikenberry, G. John. 1988. "Conclusion: An Institutional Approach to American Foreign Economic Policy." In *The State and American Foreign Economic Policy,* edited by G. John Ikenberry, David Lake, and Michael Matsanduno, 219–43. Cornell University Press, Ithaca.

Immergut, Ellen. 1990. "Institutions, Veto Points, and Policy Results: A Comparative Analysis of Health Care." *Journal of Public Policy* 10(4): 391–416.

——. 1992. *Health Politics: Interests and Institutions in Western Europe.* Cambridge University Press, New York.

Intal, Ponciano, Jr., Melanie Milo, Celia Reyes, and Leilanie Basilio. 1998. "The Philippines." In *East Asia in Crisis: From Being a Miracle to Needing One?* edited by Ross McLeod and Ross Garnaut, 145–61. Routledge, London.

International Monetary Fund (IMF). 1999a. *Financial Sector Crisis and Restructuring: Lessons From Asia.* International Monetary Fund, Washington, D.C.

——. 1999b. *IMF-Supported Programs in Indonesia, Korea, and Thailand: A Preliminary Assessment.* International Monetary Fund, Washington, D.C.

Jayasuriya, Kanishka. 1999. "Introduction: A Framework for the Analysis of Legal Institutions in East Asia." In *Law, Capitalism and Power in Asia: The Rule of Law and Legal Institutions,* edited by Kanishka Jayasuriya, 1–27. Routledge, London.

Jesudason, James. 1989. *Ethnicity and the Economy: The State, Chinese Business, and Multinationals in Malaysia.* Oxford University Press, Singapore.

——. 1999. "The Resilience of the Dominant Parties of Malaysia and Singapore." In *The Awkward Embrace: The Dominant Party and Democracy in Mexico, South Africa, Malaysia and Taiwan,* edited by Hermann Giliomee and Charles Simkins, 127–72. Harwood Academic Publishers, Amsterdam.

Johnson, Chalmers. 1982. *MITI and the Japanese Miracle: The Growth of Industrial Policy, 1925–75.* Stanford University Press, Stanford.

Jomo K. S. 1998a. "Malaysia: From Miracle to Debacle." In *Tigers in Trouble: Financial Governance, Liberalisation and crises in East Asia,* edited by Jomo K. S., 181–94. Zed Books, London.

——. 1998b. "Malaysian Debacle: Whose Fault?" *Cambridge Journal of Economics* 22(5): 707–22.

——, ed. 1998c. *Tigers in Trouble: Financial Governance, Liberalisation, and Crises in East Asia.* Zed Books, London.

———, ed. 2001. *Malaysian Eclipse: Economic Crisis and Recovery.* Zed Books, London.

Juoro, Umar. 1998. "Indonesia." In *Political Party Systems and Democratic Development in East and Southeast Asia,* edited by Wolfgang Sachsenroder and Ulrike Frings, Vol. 1, 194–225. Ashgate, Aldershot.

Jurado, Gonzalo. 1998. "Global Capital: The Philippines in the Regional Currency Crisis." *Public Policy* 1(2): 16–50.

Kahler, Miles. 1999. "Evolution, Choice, and International Change." In *Strategic Choice and International Relations,* edited by David Lake and Robert Powell, 165–96. Princeton University Press, Princeton.

Kahn, Joel, ed. 1998. *Southeast Asian Identities: Culture and the Politics of Representation in Indonesia, Malaysia, Singapore, and Thailand.* St. Martin's Press, New York.

Kasuya, Yuko. 1999. "Presidential Connection: Parties and Party Systems in the Philippines." Graduate School of International Relations & Pacific Studies, University of California, San Diego, unpublished paper.

Katzenstein, Peter. 1976. "International Relations and Domestic Structures: Foreign Economic Policies of Advanced Industrial States." *International Organization* 30(winter): 1–45.

———, ed. 1978. *Between Power and Plenty: Foreign Economic Policies of Advanced Industrial States.* University of Wisconsin Press, Madison.

———. 1988. *Policy and Politics in West Germany: The Growth of a Semisovereign State.* Temple University Press, Philadelphia.

Kelly, David, and Anthony Reid, eds. 1998. *Asian Freedoms: The Idea of Freedom in East and Southeast Asia.* Cambridge University Press, Melbourne.

Khoo Boo Tiek. 1995. *Paradoxes of Mahathirism: An Intellectual Biography of Mahathir Mohamad.* Oxford University Press, Singapore.

———. 2000. "Unfinished Crises: Malaysian Politics in 1999." In *Southeast Asian Affairs 2000,* 165–83. Institute of Southeast Asian Affairs, Singapore.

King, Dwight. 1999. "The Debate over Electoral Reform in Indonesia." Paper presented to the Fifty-first Annual Meeting of the Association for Asian Studies, 12 March, Boston.

Knight, Jack. 1992. *Institutions and Social Conflict.* Cambridge University Press, New York.

Knight, Jack, and Itai Sened, eds. 1995. *Explaining Social Institutions.* University of Michigan Press, Ann Arbor.

Krasner, Stephen. 1978. *Defending the National Interest: Raw Materials Investments and U.S. Foreign Policy.* Princeton University Press, Princeton.

———. 1984. "Approaches to the State: Alternative Conceptions and Historical Dynamics." *Comparative Politics* 16: 223–44.

Kydland, Finn, and Edward Prescott. 1977. "Rules Rather than Discretion: The Inconsistency of Optimal Plans." *Journal of Political Economy* 85(3): 473–90.

Lauridsen, Laurids. 1998. "Thailand: Causes, Conduct, Consequences." In

Tigers in Trouble: Financial Governance, Liberalisation, and Crises in East Asia, edited by Jomo K. S., 137–61. Zed Books, London.

Laver, Michael, and Norman Schofield. 1991. *Multiparty Government: The Politics of Coalition in Europe.* Oxford University Press, Oxford.

Leones, Errol, and Miel Moraleda. 1998. "Philippines." In *Political Party Systems and Democratic Development in East and Southeast Asia,* edited by Wolfgang Sachsenroder and Ulrike Frings, Vol. 1, 289–342. Ashgate, Aldershot.

Levy, Brian, and Pablo Spiller, eds. 1996. *Regulations, Institutions, and Commitment: Comparative Studies of Telecommunications.* Cambridge University Press, New York.

Liddle, R. William. 2001. "Indonesia's Democratic Transition: Playing by the Rules." In *The Architecture of Democracy,* edited by Andrew Reynolds, 377–99. Oxford University Press, Oxford.

Lijphart, Arend. 1984. *Democracies: Patterns of Majoritarian and Consensus Government in Twenty-One Countries.* Yale University Press, New Haven.

———. 1992. *Parliamentary versus Presidential Government.* Oxford University Press, Oxford.

———. 1994. *Electoral Systems and Party Systems: A Study of Twenty-Seven Democracies, 1945–1990.* Oxford University Press, New York.

———. 1999. *Patterns of Democracy: Government Forms and Performance in Thirty-Six Countries.* Yale University Press, New Haven.

Lim, Joseph. 1998. "The Philippines and the East Asian Economic Turmoil." In *Tigers in Trouble: Financial Governance, Liberalisation, and Crises in East Asia,* edited by Jomo K. S., 199–221. Zed Books, London.

Linz, Juan, and Arturo Valenzuela. 1994. *The Failure of Presidential Democracy.* Johns Hopkins University Press, Baltimore.

Lukauskas, Arvid, and Francisco Rivera-Batiz, eds. 2001. *Tigers in Distress: The Political Economy of the East Asian Crisis and Its Aftermath.* Edward Elgar, London.

MacIntyre, Andrew. 1991. *Business and Politics in Indonesia.* Allen and Unwin, Sydney.

———. 1992. "Politics and the Reorientation of Economic Policy in Indonesia." In *The Dynamics of Economic Policy Reform in Southeast Asia and the Southwest Pacific,* edited by Andrew MacIntyre and Kanishka Jayasuriya, 138–57. Oxford University Press, Singapore.

———, ed. 1994. *Business and Government in Industrialising Asia.* Cornell University Press, Ithaca.

———. 1999a. "Political Institutions and the Economic Crisis in Thailand and Indonesia." In *The Politics of the Asian Economic Crisis,* edited by T. J. Pempel, 143–62. Cornell University Press, Ithaca.

———. 1999b. "Political Parties, Accountability, and Economic Governance in Indonesia." In *Democracy, Governance, and Economic Performance: East and Southeast Asia in the 1990s,* edited by Ian Marsh, Jean Blondel, and Takashi Inoguchi, 261–86. United Nations University Press, Tokyo.

——. 2001a. "Institutions and Investors: The Politics of the Financial Crisis in Southeast Asia." *International Organization* 55(1): 81–122.

——. 2001b. "Investment, Property Rights, and Corruption in Indonesia." In *Corruption: The Boom and Bust of East Asia,* edited by J. Edgardo Campos. Ateneo University Press, Manila.

MacIntyre, Andrew, and Kanishka Jayasuriya, eds. 1992. *The Dynamics of Economic Policy Reform in South-East Asia and the South-West Pacific.* Oxford University Press, Singapore.

Madison, James, Alexander Hamilton, and John Jay. 1961. *Federalist Papers.* Penguin, New York.

Magno, Alexander. 1998. "Between Populism and Reform: Facing the Test of May 1998." In *Southeast Asian Affairs 1998,* 199–212. Institute of Southeast Asian Studies, Singapore.

Mainwaring, Scott. 1999. *Rethinking Party Systems in the Third Wave of Democratization: The Case of Brazil.* Stanford University Press, Stanford.

Mainwaring, Scott, and Timothy Scully, eds. 1995. *Building Democratic Institutions: Party Systems in Latin America.* Stanford University Press, Stanford.

Maioni, Antonia. 1997. "Parting at the Crossroads: The Development of Health Insurance in the United States and Canada." *Comparative Politics* 29:411–31.

——. 1998. *Parting at the Crossroads: The Emergence of Health Insurance in the United States and Canada.* Princeton University Press, Princeton.

Mansfield, Edward, and Jack Snyder. 1995. "Democratization and the Dangers of War." *International Security* 20(1): 5–38.

Marmor, Theodore. 1994. *Understanding Health Care Reform.* Yale University Press, New Haven.

Martin, Lisa. 1995. "The Influence of National Parliaments on European Integration." In *Politics and Institutions in an Integrated Europe,* edited by Barry Eichengreen, Jeffrey Frieden, and Jurgen von Hagen, 65–92. Springer, Berlin.

——. 2000. *Democratic Commitments: Legislatures and International Cooperation.* Princeton University Press, Princeton.

Mayhew, David. 1991. *Divided We Govern: Party Control, Law-Making, and Investigations, 1946–1990.* Yale University Press, New Haven.

McCubbins, Matthew. 1991. "Government on Lay-Away: Federal Spending and Deficits under Divided Party Control." In *The Politics of Divided Government,* edited by Gary Cox and Sam Kernell, 113–53. Westview Press, Boulder.

McLeod, Ross. 1998a. "Indonesia." In *East Asia in Crisis: From Being a Miracle to Needing One?* edited by Ross McLeod and Ross Garnaut, 31–41. Routledge, London.

——. 1998b. "The New Era of Financial Fragility." In *East Asian in Crisis: From Being a Miracle to Needing One?* edited by Ross McLeod and Ross Garnaut, 333–51. Routledge, London.

McLeod, Ross, and Ross Garnaut, eds. 1998. *East Asia in Crisis: From Being a Miracle to Needing One?* Routledge, London.

Mijares, Roy. 1999. "Philippine Resiliency to the Asian Financial Crisis." *RIM Pacific Business and Industries* 1(43): 28–40.

Miller, H. Lyman. 2000. "The Late Imperial Chinese State." In *The Modern Chinese State,* edited by David Shambaugh, 15–41. Cambridge University Press, New York.

Milne, R. S., and Diane Mauzy. 1999. *Malaysian Politics under Mahathir.* Routledge, London.

Milner, Helen. 1997. *Interests, Institutions, and Information: Domestic Politics and International Relations.* Princeton University Press, Princeton.

Montes, Manuel. 1999. "The Philippines as an Unwilling Participant in the Asian Economic Crisis." In *Asian Contagion: The Causes and Consequences of a Financial Crisis,* edited by Karl Jackson, 241–68. Westview Press, Boulder.

Montinola, Gabriella. 1999. "Parties and Accountability in the Philippines." *Journal of Democracy* 10(1): 126–40.

Montinola, Gabriella, Yingyi Qian, and Barry Weingast. 1995. "Federalism, Chinese Style: The Political Basis for Economic Success in China." *World Politics* 48(1): 50–81.

Moser, Robert. 2001. "The Consequences of Russia's Mixed-Member Electoral System." In *Mixed-Member Electoral Systems: The Best of Both Worlds?* edited by Matthew Shugart and Martin Wattenberg, 494–520. Oxford University Press, New York.

National Democratic Institute for International Affairs (NDI). 2000. *Indonesia's Road to Constitutional Reform: The 2000 MPR Annual Session.* National Democratic Institute for International Affairs, Washington, D.C.

Noble, Gregory, and John Ravenhill, eds. 2000. *The Asian Financial Crisis and the Architecture of Global Finance.* Cambridge University Press, Melbourne.

North, Douglass. 1990. *Institutions, Institutional Change, and Economic Performance.* Cambridge University Press, New York.

North, Douglass, and Robert Thomas. 1973. *The Rise of the Western World: A New Economic History.* Cambridge University Press, New York.

North, Douglass, and Barry Weingast. 1989. "Constitutions and Credible Commitments: The Evolution of the Institutions of Public Choice in 17th Century England." *Journal of Economic History* 49: 803–32.

Nukul Commission Report. 1998. *Analysis and Evaluation of Facts Behind Thailand's Economic Crisis,* English ed. The Nation, Bangkok.

Ockey, James. 1994. "Political Parties, Factions, and Corruption in Thailand." *Asian Survey* 28(2): 160–66.

———. 1997. "Thailand: The Crafting of Democracy." In *Southeast Asian Affairs 1997.* Institute of Southeast Asian Studies, Singapore.

"The Oil Deregulation Agenda." 1996. *Legislative Features* (Jan–Jun): 2–28.

Pasuk, Phongpaichit, and Chris Baker. 1998. *Thailand's Boom and Bust.* Silkworm Books, Bangkok.

———. 1999. "The Political Economy of the Thai Crisis." *Journal of the Asia Pacific Economy* 4(1): 193–208.

Pempel, T. J. 1982. *Policy and Politics in Japan: Creative Conservatism.* Temple University Press, Philadelphia.

——, ed. 1999. *The Politics of the Asian Economic Crisis.* Cornell University Press, Ithaca.

Persson, Torsten, and Guido Tabellini. 1990. *Macroeconomic Policy, Credibility and Politics.* Harwood Academic, London.

——, eds. 1994. *Monetary and Fiscal Policy.* MIT Press, Cambridge, Mass.

Pierson, Paul. 2000. "The Limits of Design: Explaining Institutional Origins and Change." *Governance* 13(4): 475–99.

Pincus, Jonathan, and Rizal Ramli. 1998. "Indonesia: From Showcase to Basket Case." *Cambridge Journal of Economics* 22(6): 723–34.

Poterba, James. 1994. "State Responses to Fiscal Crises: The Effects of Budgetary Institutions and Processes." *Journal of Political Economy* 102: 799–821.

Prudhisan, Jumbala. 1999. "Constitutional Reform Amidst Economic Crisis." In *Southeast Asian Affairs 1998,* 265–91. Institute of Southeast Asian Studies, Singapore.

Putnam, Robert. 1988. "Diplomacy and Domestic Politics: The Logic of Two-Level Games." *International Organization* 42: 427–60.

Radelet, Steven, and Jeffrey Sachs. 1998. "The East Asian Financial Crisis: Diagnosis, Remedies, Prospects." *Brookings Papers on Economic Activity,* no. 1: 1–90.

Rae, Douglas. 1971. *The Political Consequences of Electoral Laws.* Yale University Press, New Haven.

Rais, Yatim. 1995. *Freedom under Executive Power in Malaysia: A Study of Executive Supremacy.* Endowment Press, Kuala Lumpur.

Rasiah, Rajah. 1998. "Bursting the Bubble: Causes of the Southeast Asian Financial Crisis." Ms., National University of Malaysia, Kuala Lumpur, January 1998.

Raustialia, Kal. 1997. "Domestic Institutions and International Regulatory Cooperation: Comparative Responses to the Convention on Biological Diversity." *World Politics* 49: 482–509.

Reed, Steven. 1994. "Democracy and the Personal Vote: A Cautionary Tale from Japan." *Electoral Studies* 13(1): 17–28.

Riker, William. 1980. "Implications from the Disequilibrium of Majority Rule for the Study of Institutions." *American Political Science Review* 74: 432–46.

——. 1992. "The Justification of Bicameralism." *International Political Science Review* 13: 101–16.

Rivera, Temario. 1994. *Landlords and Capitalists: Class, Family, and State in Philippine Manufacturing.* University of the Philippines Press, Quezon City.

Robison, Richard. 1986. *Indonesia: The Rise of Capital.* Allen and Unwin, Sydney.

Robison, Richard, and Andrew Rosser. 1998. "Contesting Reform: Indonesia's New Order and the IMF." *World Development* 26(8): 1593–609.

Robison, Richard, Mark Beeson, Kanishka Jayasuriya, and Hyuk-Rae Kim, eds. 2000. *Politics and Markets in the Wake of the Asian Crisis.* Routledge, London.

Rocamora, Joel. 1998. "Philippine Political Parties, Electoral System and Political Reform." *Philippines International Review* 1(1).

Roeder, Philip. 1993. *Red Sunset: The Failure of Soviet Politics.* Princeton University Press, Princeton.

Rogowski, Ronald. 1999. "Institutions as Constraints on Strategic Choice." In *Strategic Choice and International Relations,* edited by David Lake and Robert Powell, 115–36. Princeton University Press, Princeton.

Root, Hilton. 1989. "Tying the King's Hands: Credible Commitments and Royal Fiscal Policy during the Old Regime." *Rationality and Society* 1(2): 240–58.

———. 1994. *The Fountain of Privilege: Political Foundations of Markets in Old Regime France and England.* University of California Press, Berkeley.

———. 1996. *Small Countries Big Lesson: Governance and the Rise of East Asia.* Oxford University Press, Hong Kong.

Roubini, Nouriel, and Jeffrey Sachs. 1989. "Political and Economic Determinants of Budgets in the Industrial Democracies." *European Economic Review* 33: 903–38.

Sachs, Jeffrey, and Andrew Warner. 1995. "Economic Convergence and Economic Policies." *National Bureau of Economic Research Working Paper,* no. 5039. National Bureau of Economic Research, Washington, D.C.

Santos, Soliman. 1997. "History of the Debate: Parliamentary versus Presidential in the Philippines." In *Shift,* edited by Soliman Santos, Florencia Abad, Joel Rocamora, and Chay Florentino-Holifena, 11–47. Ateneo Center for Social Policy and Public Affairs, Quezon City.

Sartori, Giovanni. 1976. *Parties and Party Systems: A Framework for Analysis.* Cambridge University Press, Cambridge, UK.

Schelling, Thomas. 1960. *The Strategy of Conflict.* Harvard University Press, Cambridge, Mass.

Schram, Stuart, ed. 1987. *Foundations and Limits of State Power in China.* Chinese University Press, Hong Kong.

Searle, Peter. 1999. *The Riddle of Malaysian Capitalism: Rent-Seekers or Real Capitalists?* Allen and Unwin, Sydney.

Shepsle, Kenneth. 1991. "Discretion, Institutions, and the Problem of Commitment." In *Social Theory for a Changing Society,* edited by Pierre Bourdieu and James Coleman, 245–62. Westview Press, Boulder.

Shirk, Susan. 1992. *The Political Logic of Economic Reform in China.* University of California Press, Berkeley.

Shugart, Matthew. 1998. "The Inverse Relationship between Party Strength and Executive Strength: A Theory of Politician's Constitutional Choices." *British Journal of Political Science* 28(1): 1–29.

———. 2001. "Sistemas de Gobierno en América Latina: Frenos y Contrapesos en una Era de Globalizacién." In *Democracia en Déficit: Gobernabilidad y Desarrollo en América Latina y el Caribe,* edited by Fernando Carillo, 143–87. Interamerican Development Bank, Washington, D.C.

Shugart, Matthew, and John Carey. 1992. *Presidents and Assemblies: Constitutional Design and Electoral Dynamics.* Cambridge University Press, New York.

Shugart, Matthew, and Scott Mainwaring, eds. 1997. *Presidentialism and Democracy in Latin America.* Cambridge University Press, New York.

Shugart, Matthew, and Martin Wattenberg. 2001a. "Conclusion: Are Mixed-Member Systems the Best of Both Worlds?" In *Mixed-Member Electoral Systems: The Best of Both Worlds?* edited by Matthew Shugart and Martin Wattenberg, 571–98. Oxford University Press, New York.

———, eds. 2001b. *Mixed-Member Electoral Systems: The Best of Both Worlds?* Oxford University Press, New York.

Sicat, Gerardo. 1998. "The Philippine Economy in the Asian Crisis." *ASEAN Economic Bulletin* 15(3): 290–96.

Sidel, John. 1999a. *The Beginning of the End or the End of the Beginning?: Crises, Cycles, and Sea-Changes in Fin-de-Siecle Southeast Asia.* School of Oriental and African Studies, London. Mimeographed.

———. 1999b. *Capital, Coercion, and Crime: Bossism in the Philippines.* Stanford University Press, Stanford.

Simandjuntak, Djisman. 1999. "An Inquiry into the Nature, Causes and Consequences of the Indonesian Crisis." *Journal of the Asia Pacific Economy* 4(1): 171–92.

Singson, Gabriel. 1998a. "The Philippines: Capitalizing on Sustained Financial Stability." Address of the Bangko Sentral ng Pilipinas at the Euromoney Conference: The Philippines in Asia—Leading in a New Investment Era, Makati City, November 11, 1998.

———. 1998b. The Philippines: From Crisis to Recovery. Address of the Bangko Sentral ng Pilipinas at the Financial Seminar Plenary Session: Pulling out of the Asian Financial Crisis, New York, April 7, 1998.

Smith, Steven, and Thomas Remington. 2001. *The Politics of Institutional Choice.* Princeton University Press, Princeton.

Soesastro, Hadi, and M. Chatib Basri. 1998. "Survey of Recent Developments." *Bulletin of Indonesian Economic Studies* 34(1): 3–54.

Steinmo, Sven. 1989. "Political Institutions and Tax Policy in the United States, Sweden, and Britain." *World Politics* 41(4): 500–535.

Stubbs, Richard. 1999. "War and Economic Development: Export-Oriented Industrialization in East and Southeast Asia." *Comparative Politics* 31(3): 337–55.

Suchit, Bunbongkarn. 1996a. "Thailand in 1995: The More Things Change, the More They Remain the Same." In *Southeast Asian Affairs 1996,* 357–68. Institute of Southeast Asian Studies, Singapore.

———. 1996b. *Thailand: The State of the Nation.* Institute of Southeast Asian Studies, Singapore.

Suehiro, Akira. 1989. *Capital Accumulation in Thailand 1855–1985.* Centre for East Asian Cultural Studies, Tokyo.

Sukma, Rizal. 1998. "Indonesia: A Year of Politics and Sadness." In *Southeast Asian Affairs 1998,* 105–23. Institute of Southeast Asian Affairs, Singapore.

Sundquist, James. 1992. *Constitutional Reform and Effective Government.* Brookings Institution, Washington, D.C.

Surbakti, Ramlan. 1999. "Formal Political Institutions." In *Indonesia: The Challenge of Change,* edited by Richard Baker, Hadi Soesastro, J. Kristiadi, and Douglas Ramage, 59–80. Institute of Southeast Asian Studies, Singapore.

Surin, Maisirikrod. 1997. "The Making of Thai Democracy: A Study of Political Alliances among the State, the Capitalists, and the Middle Class." In *Democratization in Southeast Asia,* edited by L. Anek, 141–66. Institute of Southeast Asian Studies, Singapore.

Suthy, Prasartsert. 1995. "The Rise of the NGOs as a Critical Social Movement in Thailand." *Asian Exchange Biannual Bulletin of the Asian Regional Exchange for New Alternatives* 11(2): 75–108.

Thelen, Kathleen. 1999. "Historical Institutionalism in Comparative Politics." *Annual Review of Political Science* 2(1): 369–404.

Timberman, David, ed. 1998. *The Philippines: New Directions in Domestic Policy and Foreign Relations.* The Asia Society, New York.

Tongchai, Winichakul. 1994. *Siam Mapped: A History of the Geo-Body of a Nation.* University of Hawaii Press, Honolulu.

Tsebelis, George. 1995. "Decision Making in Political Systems: Veto Players in Presidentialism, Parliamentarism, Multicameralism, and Mulitpartyism." *British Journal of Political Science* 25(3): 289–325.

——. 2000. "Veto Players and Institutional Analysis." *Governance* 13(4): 441–74.

Tsebelis, George, and Jeannette Money. 1997. *Bicameralism.* Cambridge University Press, New York.

Tuano, Philip. 1998. "Oil Deregulation: Searching for the Right Solution." *Politik* 4(3): 9–12.

Valenzuela, Arturo. 1991. "The Military in Power: The Consolidation of One Man Rule." In *The Struggle for Democracy in Chile, 1984–90,* edited by P. Drake and I. Jaksic, 21–72. University of Nebraska Press, Lincoln.

Velasco, Renato. 1999. "The Philippines." In *Democracy, Governance, and Economic Performance: East and Southeast Asia,* edited by Ian Marsh, Jean Blondel and Takash Inoguchi, 167–202. United Nations University Press, Tokyo.

Wade, Robert. 1990. *Governing the Market: Economic Theory and the Role of Government in East Asian Industrialization.* Princeton University Press, Princeton.

Wade, Robert, and Frank Veneroso. 1998. "The Asian Crisis: The High Debt Model vs. the Wall Street-Treasury-IMF Complex." *New Left Review* 228 (March–April): 3–22.

Warr, Peter. 1998. "Thailand." In *East Asia in Crisis: From Being a Miracle to Needing One?* edited by Ross McLeod and Ross Garnaut, 49–65. Routledge, London.

Weaver, R. Kent, and Bert A. Rockman. 1993. *Do Institutions Matter?: Government Capabilities in the United States and Abroad.* Brookings Institution, Washington, D.C.

Weingast, Barry. 1993. "Constitutions as Governance Structures: The Political Foundations of Secure Markets." *Journal of Institutional and Theoretical Economics* 149(1): 286–311.

———. 1998. "Political Stability and Civil War: Institutions, Commitment, and American Democracy." In *Analytic Narratives,* edited by Robert Bates, Avner Greif, Margaret Levi, Jean-Laurent Rosenthal, and Barry Weingast, 148–93. Princeton University Press, Princeton.

Weiss, Meredith. 2000. "The 1999 Malaysian General Elections: Issues, Insults, and Irregularities." *Asian Survey* 40(3): 413–35.

Williamson, Oliver. 1985. *The Economic Institutions of Capitalism: Firms, Markets, Relational Contracting.* Yale University Press, New Haven.

Wilson, Woodrow. 1885. *Congressional Government: A Study in American Politics.* Meridian Books, New York.

Woo, Jung-En. 1991. *Race to the Swift: State and Finance in Korean Industrialization.* Columbia University Press, New York.

Woo-Cummings, Meredith, ed. 1999. *The Developmental State.* Cornell University Press, Ithaca.

World Bank. 1997. *World Development Report 1997: The State in a Changing World.* Oxford University Press, New York.

———. 1998a. *Assessing Aid: What Works, What Doesn't, and Why.* Oxford University Press, New York.

———. 1998b. *East Asia: The Road to Recovery.* World Bank, Washington, D.C.

———. 1998c. *Indonesia in Crisis: A Macroeconomic Update.* World Bank, Washington, D.C.

World Bank, and National Economic and Social Development Board. 1998. *Competitiveness and Sustainable Economic Recovery in Thailand.* World Bank and National Economic and Social Development Board, Bangkok.

Yoshihara, Kunio. 1988. *The Rise of Ersatz Capitalism in South-East Asia.* Oxford University Press, Singapore.

Zysman, John. 1983. *Governments, Markets, and Growth: Financial Systems and the Politics of Industrial Change.* Cornell University Press, Ithaca.

Index

Indonesia *(cont.)*
House of Representatives (DPR), 48,
138–40, 144–48, 152–53
legislative bargaining on political reform, 140–48
monetary policy, 92–98
party system, 48–49, 99, 139–44,
148, 152–53, 153n
People's Consultative Assembly
(MPR), 140–48, 152–53
policy volatility, 91, 95–96, 98, 148
presidency, 48, 139, 141–42, 144–45,
148, 152–53
public support for political reform,
138, 140–42, 145, 147–48, 156
trade reform, 94, 98
veto players, 48–52, 91, 95, 99, 148–
49, 152–54, 153n
Institutions, 1–2, 105–6
and advanced industrial democracies,
6–7, 158, 163, 165
and developing countries, 1, 5–8,
163, 165
limits of analysis of, 11, 49–51, 101–
2, 154–55, 159, 166–67
theories about change in, 10–11,
105–8, 157n, 157–59, 157n,
161–63
theories about governance and, 2,
17–27
Italy, 40, 158

Japan, 12, 40, 54, 150n

Kasuya, Yuko, 45n, 169n
Katzenstein, Peter, 17n, 24
Korea, South, 102, 102n, 150n
Krasner, Stephen, 25
Kuhonta, Erik, 169n

Legal systems, 5–7, 168
Lijphart, Arend, 26n, 46n

Mahathir Mohamad, 48–49, 80–90,
132–37
Mainwaring, Scott, 6n
Malaysia
ethnic cleavages, 47, 134–36, 135n
152, 159

exchange rate management, 81, 89
financial sector reform, 82–88
fiscal policy, 81–88
monetary policy, 81–88
party system, 46–47, 136
policy volatility, 80, 83–84, 87–88, 90
potential for political change, 136–37
pressures for political change, 131–
37
reformasi, 133
veto players, 45–48, 49–52, 79, 82,
136, 151–52, 154
Mayhew, David, 26n
MCA, 46n, 137
McCubbins, Matthew, 23n, 26n, 28
Megawati Sukarnoputri, 139, 146
Mexico, 42, 151n
Montinola, Gabriella, 45n

National political architecture, 1, 4, 5–
8, 30, 35–36, 38–39, 42–49, 51–
52, 149–55
optimality, 162–64
See also Indonesia; Malaysia; Philippines; Thailand
New Aspiration Party, 43, 50, 112, 113,
117, 121
New Zealand, 7, 158
North, Douglass, 19–20, 106

Party systems, 6, 25, 25n, 40, 42
in Indonesia, 48–49, 99, 139–48,
152–53, 153n
in Malaysia, 46n, 46–48, 50, 136
in the Philippines, 44–45, 50
in Thailand, 43–44, 50, 109–10,
118–19, 149–51
PAS, 135
Philippines
central bank, 72–74
congressional opposition to constitutional change, 124, 129–30,
155–56
financial sector reform, 73–74
fiscal policy, 74–75
legislative bargaining and policy delay,
70–71, 75–76, 78–79, 125
monetary policy, 72–73
oil sector deregulation, 76–79,

Cornell Studies in Political Economy

A series edited by PETER J. KATZENSTEIN